My Journey to Grace

To Grace

Shattering Mainstream Illusions & Creating My Desired Life

Dr. Lynn Carey

BALBOA.PRESS
A DIVISION OF HAY HOUSE

Balboa Press books may be ordered through booksellers or by contacting:

Balboa Press
A Division of Hay House
1663 Liberty Drive
Bloomington, IN 47403
www.balboapress.com
844-682-1282

Because of the dynamic nature of the Internet, any web addresses or links contained in this book may have changed since publication and may no longer be valid. The views expressed in this work are solely those of the author and do not necessarily reflect the views of the publisher, and the publisher hereby disclaims any responsibility for them.

The author of this book does not dispense medical advice or prescribe the use of any technique as a form of treatment for physical, emotional, or medical problems without the advice of a physician, either directly or indirectly. The intent of the author is only to offer information of a general nature to help you in your quest for emotional and spiritual well-being. In the event you use any of the information in this book for yourself, which is your constitutional right, the author and the publisher assume no responsibility for your actions.

Any people depicted in stock imagery provided by Getty Images are models, and such images are being used for illustrative purposes only. Certain stock imagery © Getty Images.

Print information available on the last page.

ISBN: 978-1-9822-5513-8 (sc)
ISBN: 978-1-9822-5515-2 (hc)
ISBN: 978-1-9822-5514-5 (e)

Library of Congress Control Number: 2020917999

Balboa Press rev. date: 09/17/2020

CONTENTS

Creating My Desired Life Became My Journey to Grace vii

Chapter 1: My Dad...1

Chapter 2: Scoliosis...9

Chapter 3: Chiropractic 15

Chapter 4: Opening My Practice.....................................29

Chapter 5: Figuring Out Financial Freedom 49

Chapter 6: Personal Transformations...............................55

Chapter 7: Taking a New Direction 73

Chapter 8: Made It to Miami! 81

Chapter 9: Recommendations for Creating Your
             Desired Life—Pulling It All Together..............91

Recommended Books, Videos, and other Sources..............99

CREATING MY DESIRED LIFE BECAME MY JOURNEY TO GRACE

From the time I was a child, I had a deep knowing that there had to be more to life besides what I was being shown. I felt a deep desire for more and a strong urge to help or *save* everyone else too. I was like a child asking why. However, the adults in my life did not have answers to many of my questions. They seemed annoyed when I asked. I decided to just be quiet, do what I had to do, be a good girl, and not cause any trouble until I could make decisions for myself. Unfortunately for me, I believed it when I was told continuously that to be successful in life, you had to get a college education. I thought that would lead me to become an adult who could make my own decisions. I dreamed maybe that was the light at the end of the tunnel.

I worried about everything. I became a perfectionist in my attempt to do what was right and to get others' approval. That perfectionism created a lot of pain physically and emotionally. Finding happiness was never discussed once; it was all about working hard. In fact, doing anything besides work was not really accepted. No one around me had fun. If others were having fun, it was criticized and judged: "It must be nice" or "I don't know how they can afford that!" I was wondering what the point of all this hard work was since it never seemed to be enough.

This asking *why* inside myself has led me to one of the greatest journeys, I call my life, and it keeps getting better. I have learned to step outside what the world calls normal and find my own bliss. The greatest peace and freedom you can ever give yourself is to truly find that space within and then learn to create it without. That is the journey I am going to share with you. It is a story of my opinions, viewpoints, and preferences. It is in no way stating this is the right way or the only way, but the intent is to share another perspective. I feel that we have been programmed to see life a certain way, and those programs limit our perceptions. What if we had a broader view? By finding a broader view and stepping outside the mainstream narratives, I found my greatest understanding and joy. I know in my heart that we can be, do, or have anything we want. We are here to create heaven on earth. Your bliss can be found every day. My bliss is my new normal.

I do not want to be politically correct. I do not want to be right. I want to break down the barriers of societal thinking to start a conversation. I want to inspire a generation to think for themselves, to create the best version of themselves, and to become empowered leaders in their own lives. Only when everyone reclaims their joy, happiness, health, purpose, wealth, and mind-set can we truly have peace on earth.

CHAPTER 1

MY DAD

My parents were married for twenty years before I came along. For some reason, my mom could not have a baby; after trying with the help of the medical world, without any luck, she gave up. When she found out she was pregnant with me, she thought she was going through early menopause at age forty-one. This was in the early seventies when it was not so common to have a baby in your forties. The medical doctor scared her to death about everything that could go wrong with having a baby at her age. My mom said she left his office crying. She was in shock, not knowing if she should be happy or sad. I find this incredibly heartbreaking that a medical doctor took my mom's joy away that day. My mom worries about a lot anyway. I think that is her normal vibration. So, I learned how to worry more so that I could soothe her; in turn, if she was soothed, I was soothed. This pattern probably started with me in the womb.

I never felt heard as a child. I discovered later in life that

I created drama in my life that would keep me in patterns of stress and worry. Only if I was really stressed out could I be heard, at least somewhat. The one person I remember always listening to me was my dad. I had terrible anxiety about going to school. The first day of preschool, my dad brought me, and I hung onto his leg, crying for him not to leave me. I still remember that. My mom listened to the teacher, who told her to force me to stay because I needed to get socialized with other kids. Now as an adult, I say, "No I didn't." They should have brought me home. First thing I learned from that experience is that your voice, your opinions, and your feelings do not matter. How many kids does this happen to today? We are trained from the start that our voice does not matter. But our voice is where our power is.

In grade school, the nightmare continued. Here is where my worrying about everything took off. I took every book home with me every night. I wanted to give my all to homework, not forget anything, and make sure I was prepared for the next day. I got a lot of homework. How cruel too? After sitting all day watching the clock, praying to get through another day of torture, I had to go home and do more work. And for me, worry some more.

In math, I got about fifty problems a night to reinforce the class lesson. My dad would see how distraught I felt. He would say, "Show me you can do the first ten problems, and I will do the rest." I did the first ten, and then my dad would look over my shoulder for the next forty and spout off the answers as I quickly wrote them.

I went to Catholic school for twelve years. There were some nasty nuns and lay people who taught in those institutions. They truly treated us like animals. They got off on themselves being in power. They probably did not like themselves, let alone children. My grade school principal was one of the evilest nuns I have ever met. May they burn in the hell they preach. I do not believe in a hell we go to but a hell we can create while in this physical body. She did a great job of that. I was an A/B student. I studied hard and behaved. I sat in the classroom, upset about the same kids who always got into trouble. I was always on the honor roll. I somehow was well liked. I knew how to put on a happy face and be kind to others amid the pain I felt inside.

It never surprises me when I hear that a student who had everything going for him or her committed suicide. They are the ones who had enough of the system. I wanted to die every day. I am concerned for the ones who never question it and then put their kids through the same thing. When I really got scared or upset by a teacher who I had to deal with daily, I told my dad. He would go talk to them to see why we had so much homework and what was going on. He never got many answers. I do recall one teacher telling him he was the only parent who complained of too much homework. Many other parents thought their kids did not get enough. I am sure they were the parents of the same kids who got in trouble every day. What a disconnect. As my dad tried to fight for me, he lost his own battle with life.

My dad looked older. I got embarrassed when kids at my school thought he was my grandfather. Now I know that it was because my dad was so beat up by life that his energy was slowly dwindling. My dad was an entrepreneur at heart. Before I came along, he tried and failed at many businesses. The last business was a shoe store. I recall going to that shoe store. I was just a toddler. I know that he lost that business, and he was out of work.

I did not understand the dynamic at the time, but I have come to understand how I carried this energy with me most of my life. A friend had a connection at a bakery and got my dad a job. He had to work the night shift. He began getting home from work in the morning when I was getting up to go to school. My mom had a day job working in an office in the human resources department. She also worked most evenings at her father's store and on Saturdays. She seemed happy just to be working and busy. My mom would say that as long as we have our health, we can always get money. I think she was wrong. I think health and money are very connected. It is about having happiness in your life, doing a job that you find purposeful, and having the time to heal, to be, and to enjoy life. Money gives you freedom of choice.

My dad wanted meaning and purpose. He would sleep all day while I was in school, pick me up from school, help me with my homework, and we would get dinner. Then he would be off to work again. What kind of life is that? I was being shown the definition of the term *rat race*, but I did not come to understand it until much later. One day, my dad's body finally started to give out to the point that he could not ignore it anymore. My mom begged him to go to the doctor. He did not want to go. He used to install televisions in hospitals, and I think he knew that medical intervention could make you sick.

Some people would say, "Oh, if he just went to the doctor sooner, he could have been saved." I disagree. Keep reading, and you will see a new perspective. My dad ended up going to the doctor because the pain in his leg prevented him from going to work. He was admitted to the hospital immediately because they found a blood clot in his leg. Once in the hospital, they discovered cancer in his lungs. The story was that my dad was a heavy smoker, so the cigarettes killed him. However, my maternal grandfather died smoking, drinking, and eating a bad diet while working in his own store until he was eighty-six years old.

My dad was diagnosed in May 1986. I watched my poor father lose the fight of his life. He went through chemotherapy, radiation, and surgery, all to just wither away. I had to help my mom move him to a chair just to change the bedsheets. His legs were as skinny as mine, and I was twelve. Finally, the doctor told him that there was nothing more they could do for him. This is a crime in itself because they have no right to play God. They filled him with poisons, cut out body parts, did nothing about changing his lifestyle, then just left him to die. The doctor told him he had only so much time to live.

My mom told me he made her drive him around for a while before coming home because he could not bear to face me. I did get the chance to talk with my dad about my life plans. We sat on the couch, and I shared with him that I planned to start working that summer. When I turned thirteen, I would work at my grandfather's store to save to buy a car by the time I was sixteen. I also planned to go to college, and maybe I would have a career in business. I told him I would be successful. I did not want him to worry about me.

My dad eventually became bedridden. He would ask me to play his favorite song by Stevie Wonder, "I Just Called to Say I Love You." He asked me to play it repeatedly. I had a cassette tape, and I would hit play and rewind over and over again on my little pink boom box. Eventually, my dad fell into a coma. He died on February 21, 1987, at the age of fifty-three.

The only time I remember crying during the funeral services was when I had to follow the casket down the church aisle for the mass, with everyone there, including my classmates, watching. How awful. Who thinks of these rituals? I cried more watching him suffer before he died. Some part of me was relieved when he died because I knew he was not suffering anymore. I do know that my life's perspective completely changed. I had one parent in heaven and one parent on earth. All I really wanted was to join my dad in heaven because I knew he left me in hell on earth. What are we doing here? Now the inner feeling that there had to be more to life was stronger than ever.

After the services, we continued like normal, but life was never normal again. I went to school every day and started working that summer, just like I told my dad. My mom continued to work her two jobs. I was old enough now to stay home by myself. I recently found my report card from that seventh-grade year. I was absent only two days and still had all As and two Bs. So sad. When was there time to grieve? All I was taught was working hard solves everything. I think we find that in the American culture. Maybe the system needs to be revamped if we keep working and never have enough. What are we working for?

There was one teacher I adored from third grade. She was young and kind. She was engaged when she taught me. By the time my dad died, she was married and had a two-year-old and a four-year-old. She wrote me the most beautiful letter after my dad passed, telling me she was there to talk to if I needed her. Sadly, she died two weeks later. She was privately suffering from her own battle with lupus. She was only twenty-eight years old. Life just seemed cruel and unjust. I kept praying.

Fast-forward twenty years later. I ended up being an entrepreneur like my father. It was 2008, and the entire market was collapsing. I had my own practice as a chiropractor, had rental properties, and a toddler. My cash flow could not keep up with the bills rapidly coming in. I could not sell or refinance any of my properties with the state of the economy. I realized this was exactly what my dad had experienced. I did not have a partner whom I could turn to for any emotional support. It was a rarefied person who understood what I was going through. I had so much compassion for my dad at that moment. I felt the weight of these pressures, and it was heavy. It is so important to have the right people around you when you hit these times in life, especially when going for your dreams. I really believe it can make you or break you. Lucky for me, I had already had my own healing journey. I had discovered grace.

CHAPTER 2

SCOLIOSIS

The following summer when I was getting ready to enter high school, I was looking at myself in the mirror. I noticed I lost the waistline curve on my left side, and I felt a big bump on that side. I asked my mom if she saw anything on my back. She became upset seeing the prominent muscle protrusion. She called for an appointment with my pediatrician. The doctor told us I had scoliosis and referred me to one of the top hospitals. I was already confused. I thought, *Isn't that the thing I was checked for a few times in school when I had to wear my bathing suit uncomfortably under my school uniform? They always said I was okay! How could they have missed this bump? It was very prominent!* The orthopedic doctor said my scoliosis was severe. It measured fifty-six degrees from the center of my back. He ordered me to get fitted for a scoliosis brace. I was supposed to wear it twenty-three hours out of every twenty-four hours each day. *What? I just got the braces off my teeth. This is ten times worse.*

The brace was as hard as a plastic bowl. It wrapped around

my torso. It reached from under my armpits to the top of my hips. I wore a man's undershirt underneath to catch the sweat and to try to protect my skin from the cuts that started appearing under my armpits. The doctor told me I would have to wear the brace for the next five years because I was not done growing. I was fourteen. I had not begun menstruation. Even beyond that, it would take a couple years to solidify the maturing process. We had a family friend refer us to another prominent orthopedic doctor. This guy had such a charismatic bedside manner. He was very comforting. He told me it would be okay to wear the brace only twelve hours of each day. Twelve hours sounded much better than twenty-three. Now this brace was added to the hell I felt I was already living in.

I went to an all-girls Catholic high school. I decided to wear the brace underneath my school uniform. It fit, and it would be worse wearing it to work after school. I felt stressed working at my job after school, but I felt it was important to earn my own money. I did not feel I had many options at that age to choose a different job. Happiness was not mentioned, only hard work, so I thought I was doing the right thing. I had someone I looked up to tell me that work is work, and the grass is not greener on the other side. I felt stuck. When I would complain about school to my mom, she would tell me, "Wait until you get out; you'll wish you were back in school. School years are the best years of your life." *What? It gets worse than this? What are we doing here?* I questioned classes such as algebra, precalculus, physics, and English literature. We read *Romeo and Juliet.* Why? My mom, of course, would chime in, "You'll see. You'll need it." I have been out of high school for more than twenty-five years. I still have not needed it. I had a difficult time making sense of it all. I maintained my honor roll status. I continued to work part-time. I methodically saved half my paycheck every week for my future car. It felt like daily madness.

By the following spring, on one of my periodic checkups to my doctor for scoliosis, he told me I would be a good candidate for the Harrington rod surgery. I went for second opinions. Unfortunately, they were all orthopedic doctors, all cut from the same cloth. The surgery sounded great because, after six months, I would be done with the brace for good. We scheduled the surgery for that summer. Heaven forbid I disrupt my school year; we were learning so many important things.

It was scheduled for August 18, 1989. It was late in the summer because I had to give my own blood ahead of time, which took several weeks. If I needed a blood transfusion during the procedure, it was better to use my own blood. This was during the HIV crisis. The night before my surgery, my mom had already gone home, and the nurse came in to prep me for the next morning. She proceeded to tell me all the horrible risks that could happen during surgery. *What? Where was this discussion a few months ago?* I tried to shut it from my mind and go to sleep. They took me to surgery at 6:00 a.m.

After the surgery, I woke up in the ICU with tubes down my throat, in my arm, and up my crotch so I could pee. They sedated me to lay flat on my back the first few days. Afterward, I was moved to a regular room, where I continued to get a morphine needle injected into my thighs every few hours to numb the pain. The top of my thighs turned black and blue from the constant shots. The nurse had to roll me onto my side on a regular rotation. She also had to bathe me in bed.

Then they came to get me because I had to get fitted for a new brace. *What?* I was told that the old one would not fit because my spinal curve had been reduced. They proceeded to lay me on a narrow band. It went along my freshly cut spinal incision. I hung in the air with my legs in stirrups and my arms around two nurses' necks as they supported me. I screamed and cried in horrendous pain! I remember almost choking the nurse's neck with my arm as she winced, saying she was so sorry. No amount of morphine covered up the pain from having my entire body weight lie on my newly cut spinal incision. This was how they plastered my body to make a mold for my new brace. It was definitely the worst part.

Gradually, I began to get up and learned to walk again on my own. It was a great accomplishment when I made it down the hall, holding onto the side rail. I do remember lying in that hospital bed, thinking that being there was better than my life. I did not have to be at the job I hated. I could relax without feeling guilty. I see this happen to so many people. Many do not realize that never addressing the silent pain of their daily life can manifest as disease. The subconscious will choose for you. Disease is a huge distraction that causes you to wake up. It may be the only thing that forces you to make a change. I was let out of the hospital within ten days. That was the end of August. Oh, and I made the first day of school for my tenth-grade year, right after Labor Day. I never let the ball drop.

I began the new school year still wearing the brace for six more months, and then I gladly threw it away. My doctor told me the surgery would bring about my menstruation. He was right. It started five months later. How sick is it that we think it is okay to manipulate and invade the body? I never found normal again. I had been in emotional and mental pain before the surgery, but now I was in physical pain too. It was a gradual on-and-off thing. I never related it to my surgery. I guess every time I went to any doctor for whatever symptom I experienced, they never mentioned it either. I did buy my car when I turned sixteen in May. My first taste of freedom, but it came with a price: the slavery of having to pay for the gas, insurance, and the maintenance. These expenses were continuous, and now the job that I hated was more needed than ever.

There was always something wrong with my health. I got eyeglasses because I failed the driver's eye exam. I got a severe case of chickenpox from babysitting. I had a fever for over a week, and the chickenpox were everywhere, including my eyes. The chickenpox appeared on the one-year anniversary of my spinal surgery. Pain began in my legs, back, and neck. I think this made my surgeon suggest removing the metal Harrington rods from my spine.

My spinal processes, the small spinal bones protruding down the spinal column, were cut off between my shoulder blades through the rest of my dorsal spine. The Harrington rods were placed along the spine with metal hooks. Bone was shaved off the ilium bone in my pelvis, combined with the spinal process bone chips, and sprinkled down my spine in order to fuse it. It is normal protocol to leave these metal rods in forever. Now my surgeon was suggesting we take them out. I did not want more surgery, but I wanted the pain to go away. We scheduled it for mid-May 1991, almost two years after the initial surgery. He told me it would be simple. It was. I only remember almost fainting in the bathroom when I first got up. I went in on a Wednesday and came home on a Friday. I was back in school on Monday. The pain did not go away. I do not remember seeing that surgeon anymore.

The pain continued. I carried a pillow with me to school to help me sit at the desk. Pain down my legs was sometimes so bad I would fall in the shower. Pain in my low back. Pain in my neck. I went to physical therapy. It did not help. I took muscle relaxers. It did not help. Fatigue. Heartburn. Headaches. Bad colds. Strep throat, at one point, lasting six months, even taking antibiotics. Every time I finished one prescription, my throat would flare up badly, and they would give me another prescription. I kept asking my doctor, "Why do I keep getting sick?" He never had an answer besides writing another prescription. I went for second opinions, and none of them had an answer. This was over a period of five years until I discovered chiropractic.

I hope you can already see the pattern that doctors do not have all the answers. Many times, they will come up with conflicting solutions. Therefore, it is so important for you to gather all differing information and form your own opinion. You must start becoming your own best doctor. I notice that different treatments work differently on different people, and most the outcomes go along with each person's belief system. I find that people heal according to their beliefs. What do you believe? What beliefs form and control your life?

CHAPTER 3

CHIROPRACTIC

I made it to college, but I did not find any relief. I almost had a nervous breakdown. I was getting more depressed than ever. College was not the light at the end of the tunnel that I had envisioned so far. I attended the university, and I loaded up on general classes. I was not sure what to major in. I could not keep up with the classes, as they were much harder than high school. I found it difficult to follow what the professor taught in class and what was on the exam. I took calculus and studied hard. When it came time to take the test, the material was not even something I recognized. How could that be? What was the reasoning? I went to the professor, and she had nothing helpful to say. I spent all my time in the math tutoring center for calculus. I still ended up with a D for fall semester, so I retook it in the winter session. In winter session, calculus was so easy. I could have gotten an A with my eyes closed. I let my two friends cheat off me. I was angry. What is going on in these universities? By the way, I have never needed calculus in real life.

I was taking general classes that would count toward most majors. I felt interest in the health industry, but all I knew was the medical profession, and they were not helping me. I continued struggling with my health. I was in more pain as my stress increased. Life seemed darker. The summer following my freshman year in college, I went in with a bunch of friends on a beach house. I lived and worked there for half of the summer, until eventually my guilt became bad. I felt guilty for being so frivolous and spending any money on a beach house while my mom was working so hard to pay for my college education. The struggle, the guilt, and the physical and emotional pain were really escalating. I was terribly depressed.

When I say chiropractic saved my life on so many levels, I truly mean it. My boyfriend at the time was also trying to figure out what to major in college. His father was going to a chiropractor, and he received some information about it. He asked me what I thought about chiropractic. I thought a chiropractor was just a back doctor who gave medicine. I was not interested until he showed me the pamphlet. I just remember reading, "The power that made the body heals the body." Something came alive in me at that moment. I had never had anyone say that to me. What did that mean? I had to investigate this school. I gave one more semester at the university before I transferred to a chiropractic school eleven hours away from home. *I never even got adjusted.* The philosophy had me. I really did not understand what I was getting into. Little did I know my life was about to change in so many ways.

First thing I noticed upon my arrival at my new school was how healthy and happy everyone looked. It was the first time I saw people enjoying life. I needed to finish some undergraduate classes before I started the actual chiropractic program. There were student clubs on campus after school, where upper-class chiropractic students taught different adjusting techniques. They had been learning from chiropractors already in practice out in the field. I asked, "How does my spine get adjusted after scoliosis surgery?" Everyone went crazy. I was like an alien who just landed on earth. They could not believe they had met someone who actually had that done. Everyone wanted to learn from my case.

I found out six months later that in the first quarter of chiropractic courses, they show the Harrington rod surgery in class. The lesson was teaching how awful the medical paradigm can be. I could not watch the video. *I felt sick.* I was still in pain from mine. I am really glad I walked into that club my first month at school. These students were studying an awfully specific and scientific technique. It would have been traumatizing for me if I had just let any student practice on my spine like we did in future classes. One of the upper-class students in the club named Tom connected me with a professor who specialized in this technique. I began to see her for regular adjustments. She would not adjust my middle spine; she only adjusted my sacroiliac joints. They were very locked up. I remember getting my first adjustment, laying on my side, and I thought, *What did I get myself into?* This was different and borderline weird. However, it was the first time that anyone explained something about my health that made sense, and I loved getting adjusted. It felt amazing.

The chiropractic philosophy recognizes an innate intelligence that runs the body all the time. Innate intelligence is what chiropractors call the life force of the body. It expresses itself as energy flowing from the brain, down the spinal cord, then out the spine through the nervous system. For those messages to get out, from the brain to the body and back, from the body to the brain, the spinal passageways have to be clear. Those passageways stay clear when there is motion between every vertebral joint in the spine. This motion also keeps the disc between each vertebra healthy. I also learned that it takes time to heal. It may take as long to heal as it did the length of time it took to get sick. I knew at that point I had been sick for about five years. They tried to fuse 90 percent of my spine. *How crazy.* I was so glad I had the rods taken out. I was really starting to see all the cracks in the medical paradigm. I continued to be in pain, but I had hope. Nothing else had worked, and this was the first time I had answers.

I began attending chiropractic philosophy seminars. The founder of the school used to drop his keys on the podium in the lecture. What happens every time you drop your keys? They fall to the ground. He was demonstrating the law of gravity, and just like the law of gravity, the body's innate intelligence flows through the body. It organizes every bodily function just like the universal intelligence that makes the sun rise every morning. I learned the history of chiropractic. Dr. D.D. Palmer was a magnetic healer in Davenport, Iowa, in the late 1800s. In the year 1895, he noticed one of his patients, who could not hear, had a bone misaligned when he palpated his spine. He moved it with his hands back into place, and the man's hearing returned. Another patient had a heart problem. D.D. found a misaligned vertebra in his spine and adjusted it. The man's heart condition cleared up. Hence, chiropractic, which means the laying on of hands, was born. He opened the first chiropractic school in Davenport, Iowa, with his son, B.J. Palmer. Some of the first chiropractors were jailed for practicing medicine without a license. There are stories that they kept adjusting the people in the jail. This is what caused the schools to have to become accredited and incorporate a process for students to get licensed. Unfortunately, I believe we sold our souls in this process. Now instead of focusing more on adjusting techniques and philosophy, more classroom time went to passing four national board examinations.

We had to learn what medical doctors do except for the drugs and surgery. I really understood how different the medical viewpoint is. They look for all kinds of symptoms that the person may be expressing and then match it to a diagnosis. I took medical terminology and discovered all they do is take simple body symptoms and give them a big name, so the person has no clue what they are talking about. For example, arthritis means inflammation of the joint. Gastritis is a stomachache or an inflamed stomach. Neuralgia is nerve pain. And did you know we all have a sciatic nerve down both legs? I see so many people diagnosed with sciatica, including myself. *Gee, thanks for telling me I have one.* Is this for power? I do not know. We should be empowering people on how their body works, not fear them into disease. Disease is nothing more than dis-ease in the body with a fancy name. I realized the medical world loses sight of the whole person. They are always looking for parts that they can label, diagnose, drug, or cut out. We do not have spare parts. And our bodies have everything we need already inside ourselves to heal. We just have to believe that. We have been programmed to not trust our bodies and to have more faith in the medication, the doctor, and the system. Did you ever notice that most medications treat symptoms and then also have side effects, causing the same symptoms or worse? We take for granted the magnificence of our bodies and all that they do every moment. As you are sitting there reading this, your lungs are breathing, your heart is beating, your kidneys are working, your hair is growing, and so are your nails. You cannot possibly name all the millions of functions happening in your body right now, let alone control them consciously with your mind. There is something bigger going on here. We need to tap into it if we ever want to experience true well-being.

We learned to honor the body's expression of symptoms. Your body is so smart. If you have too many germs, bacteria, viruses, and/or cancer cells in your body, you will get a fever to burn off all the debris. *Yes, I said cancer cells.* They are just malformed or unhealthy cells. The body will raise its temperature to kill everything off, then bring it back to normal once it has cleaned house. But what does the mainstream thinking do? We take a pill to bring the fever down because we are taught it is bad. Now the poor body must work harder to not only get rid of the debris tissues but also the toxins from the pill. Most likely, after the pill wears off, the body's temperature will spike again because it was not finished cleaning out. You delayed and interfered with the process. When you get a cold, same thing; the body is getting rid of germs, bacteria, and mucus lining that does not serve it any longer. Every time you get *sick*, your body comes back healthier and stronger if you allow it to do what it must. Most people immediately grab the cold medicine. I was on medications for many years, and I always had severe symptoms. Once I understood the body's processes, I decided to detox from any medicine I was on, including the birth control pill. I started to heal. Now when I get symptoms, my body clears out very quickly. I have not been on medication for more than twenty years except for the occasional Advil when I feel the need to push myself with my life schedule.

While I was at school, I discovered a movement educating people on the dangers of vaccinations. This was in 1994. I never questioned vaccines. It was just something I got during a regular doctor visit. Once you start to wake up and ask questions, things begin to get noticeably clear. Vaccinations no longer made sense. Our bodies are so majestic. Science may have learned to put a sperm and an egg together in a petri dish, but they still cannot physically turn the sperm and egg into a baby. That is beyond our limited conscious thought. You think when a perfect little baby is born, its innate intelligence forgot to make the poisons inside the vaccine needle? Wake up, people! Where did our common sense go? This book will not waste its time stating research, but I beg you to do some research on your own. I found tons of research showing as many damages from vaccines as there are *cures*. Most of the cases of "cures" were already happening with our natural immune response by the time the vaccine cure came along. And how about all those kids damaged by vaccines? Oh, they do not put that on the news because the news is funded by big pharma, the companies who profit enormously from the patenting and selling of those vaccines!

I began to follow the National Vaccine Information Center (NVIC) started by a woman who had a child injured by a routine vaccination. She started the center to bring this awareness to the public. She had and still has a fight on her hands. My first five years in practice, I gave out her information along with the stories of so many children injured from vaccines. I regularly donated to her organization. When my life shifted from fighting the fight to living in my bliss state of awareness, I decided to stop being in the vaccine fight. I knew the choices I would make for myself, and I preferred to influence people in my daily life and in my practice on their choices. I did not want to be in a fight. I never thought the corruption was so bad that there could be mandatory vaccinations.

Unfortunately, in present time 2020, I am hearing that New

York and California passed laws for mandatory vaccinations. I thought we lived in the free country of the United States where we are supposed to have freedom of choice? I guess the mind-numbing media and big money behind the scenes is a deadly combination. New Jersey was next to pass the mandatory vaccine law. The people spoke out against it, and it did not pass. Currently, there is another fight in Colorado. They want to remove religious exemption as a reason to refuse a vaccine. Is there still hope that our voices will be heard? Are there still enough people who think for themselves? Now with the pandemic happening right now and so many people following along like sheep to the slaughterhouse, it is time to jump back into the fighting arena.

The main agenda is mandatory vaccinations with tracking chips. Do you want to get a shot with a microchip? What if this replaces a passport, so you cannot travel without being chipped? What if they can track everything about you? We are losing our freedoms in the demise that they are saving us from death. I do not know about you, but if I cannot be free, I would rather be dead. Do you want them going into your child's school and giving them vaccines without your permission? That is what is happening right now in California and New York. This is about big money and psychopathic control. I always wondered how in the world the horrific things happened under Nazism. Now I am seeing with my own eyes how quickly the entire world was shut down with people cowering over a virus. If you utterly understood how your body works, you would never be afraid of a virus. We are never taught that the body heals itself, another way the powers that be can easily step in and take control.

We learned about many things in chiropractic school that affect the body. We learned about nutrition. I decided to finish my bachelor's degree in nutrition while I was in the chiropractic program. It was another eye-opening experience. In the nutrition undergraduate program, there were some professors trained as dieticians teaching the outdated four food groups model. The chiropractors were trained on the leading edge at the time, of plant-based diets, eating organic foods, and detoxing the body. Again, this was back in 1994 before this was so trendy. I learned both schools of thought and understood the shift.

Bottom line is that the chemicals, pesticides, hormones, antibiotics, and processing that fill our food, water, and personal care products are outstanding. Our bodies are having to get rid of toxins at a pace that is staggering to even imagine. They can get rid of toxins within normal reason without a problem. However, when they are being contaminated daily by the foods we ingest and the chemicalized products we put on our skin, they cannot keep up. Our skin is our largest organ, and what you put on your skin quickly enters the bloodstream. All these toxins create inflammation in our bodies. The inflammation is the body's natural response to getting rid of toxins. When your body is being constantly loaded with toxins, your body will live in a chronic state of inflammation.

Eventually, your body begins to break down into further dis-ease and chronic disease. This leads to so many autoimmune diseases. The body starts to have chronic symptoms from digestion issues, allergies, unbalanced blood sugar, high blood pressure, headaches, joint pain, and weight gain. If our bodies break down, can you imagine how we are affecting the earth, the plants, and the animals? It is our duty to buy organic foods and clean products not only because it is better for us and the environment but to put our money into companies whose mission is to do good for the world. That is how we show support. Once your body is clear of toxic gook, you can start to feel your body's natural rhythms and cravings. I do not have a strong stance on eating animal products. Here is how I look at it: if we had to go out and kill to get our meat, it would be a lot longer of a process in how often we eat it. There would be a natural flow. Now, with the processing of it for quick production, the animal cruelty that happens is horrific. I recommend buying organic, grass-fed, cruelty-free meats and poultry. It is the hormones, antibiotics, and animal torture that is not agreeing with our systems more than the animal meat itself. Animals still eat other animals. It is part of nature.

As we begin to view the body from a natural point of view, it opens us up to how dynamic it is and how it is affected daily by our emotional and mental states. I learned some of the theories that could cause scoliosis. If the person feels pulled in two directions, the spine can go in opposing directions, forming an S-shaped curve like I had. The theory is the mother and father had differing views, or the direction of one's life is not going in the direction it wants to. There is also a theory that scoliosis can show up if one has braces on their teeth and an emotional trauma occurs. I had braces put on my teeth the same month my dad got diagnosed with cancer. I got them off the year after he died. I checked off all the boxes for every scoliosis theory. I knew what I was being shown, as life in my childhood did not make sense. I was miserable. I think on some level my mom and dad may have had opposing views in life; he just let her have her way. I felt pulled between life and death after my dad died, having a parent in each realm.

I was only beginning to scratch the surface of uncovering the amount of emotional stress I carried, how it was creating my pain, and how I had created these patterns. I was still trying to understand my physical symptoms. Looking back, I was learning on so many levels. It is quite dynamic to learn to heal yourself while surrounded by a cocoon of chiropractors. There are so many factors that affect our health. It is important that you play detective in your life, to understand what affects you.

I continued to get adjusted by the same chiropractic professor for about six months. She kept adjusting my sacroiliac joints. I think she was afraid to touch the middle of my spine. I was still going to the technique club in the evenings to learn how to palpate and feel for spinal misalignments, what we called subluxations. Subluxation literally means a state of not enough light (lux). It is an area of the spine choking off the nerve flow or life force from lack of optimal motion in a vertebral joint. I became fast friends with Tom, the upper-class student who referred me to the professor. He kept up on my healing journey, and we both began to question why she was not adjusting my entire spine. He asked, "Do you want me to check and adjust you?" I was open to it. I trusted him. I was still in awful pain. I had nothing to lose. We were following our tools to indicate a subluxation, including x-ray and an instrument called the scope that measured heat on either side of the spine. What left an impression on me was how Tom always followed what he felt with his hands when palpating my spine.

He began adjusting different areas of my spine. I noticed improvement. It was not a quick fix. It was about another year until I stabilized out of pain. Healing happens more like a roller coaster, up and down. I remember during this time, while I was sitting at a table in the snack bar area of our school, feeling good, and then I sneezed. I could not move! I could not get up from the table! We did not have cell phones then; we had pagers. Someone found Tom, and he literally carried me to an adjusting table. He got ice for my spine and got me adjusted. Eventually, he got me home, but I had to take my exams that week standing at the teacher's podium in front of the classroom because I could not sit down. These flare-ups would happen as my spine began to be awakened back to life from the suppression and trauma of the surgery. I was awakening too. Eventually, my lower back felt good the majority of the time.

Near Tom's graduation, he adjusted me for the last time, and my last lumbar vertebrae locked up, causing intense pain. I did not understand what happened. It began to occur to me that I was in terrible fear of losing my chiropractor. He did so much for me. How could I replace him? That is when I really started to connect my emotions with my symptoms. The low back area is emotionally connected to the foundation in your life: survival, money, and relationships. I began noticing anytime I had mental stress around these topics, my low back would begin to hurt or seize up.

My last year in chiropractic school, I was studying for a voluntary all-encompassing exam that would not only prepare me for the boards but also allow me to work in our student clinic as a supervisor during patient visits. I studied so hard in addition to my regular studies and clinic patient visits. This was the year I had a headache, daily, in the back of my head on the left side. I got regularly adjusted, received massages, and had a clean diet. I had been off all medications at this point for about two years. Nothing helped. Worst of all, I failed my one chance to pass the exam after a year's worth of preparation. The daily headaches began to dissipate after the exam. This alerted me to another connection between stress and dis-ease.

During this time, I had a handsome boyfriend who treated me very well. Boys and alcohol were my escapes from the stress

I felt in my life. I began this pattern around the time I was sixteen. I never took my relationships seriously. I was not one of those girls who dreamed about a wedding. I grew up seeing many unhappily married people. Most stayed married because they were Catholic, and they thought it a sin to get divorced. I used to think it was ironic how they celebrated milestone anniversaries. Should all that suffering be celebrated? It seemed to me like more of a prison sentence than a celebration. Watching my dad die, I also knew you do not always die as a couple, even if you are in love. Therefore, I wanted to learn to be okay by myself and be financially independent. I never wanted to have a man wreck my life. When I was with a nice guy, I did not even know how to accept being treated nicely. I would cause drama. I can be a real bitch and a drunken mess behind the scenes. It was the ultimate self-sabotage. I did not consciously know this at the time, but I seemed to have a pattern of self-sabotage and self-suffering.

After failing the exam, and after about six months of pretending to be casual in our dating, the nice guy asked me if we were going to be exclusive as a couple. I panicked. I casually blew off answering the question and then began causing trouble. I remember telling my roommate that I did not know why I was acting so mean. I really thought he was amazing, and we had so much fun together. *That was the problem.* I did not know how to let any fun or happiness into my life. I was wired to suffer. If life began to feel very happy, I looked for something to worry about. I was uncomfortable feeling happy and found my comfort in worry.

I went home for winter break. One morning, I woke up with my period. I began throwing up, having diarrhea, and sweating profusely. My hands and feet went numb, and I felt extremely dizzy. It lasted forty-five minutes, and then I was fine. I know this exactly because this pattern began to happen every month. The next month, it happened again when my roommate and I were traveling to a seminar. We were in the Newark, New Jersey, airport when it hit me. I ran to the bathroom, and for the next forty-five minutes, I was on the bathroom floor. You know you feel like you are dying when you lie all over the filthy bathroom floor in an airport and do not care.

This went on every month, until it subsided to every other month, for the next five years. The illusion of the medical world was broken for me. I knew if I went to see a medical doctor at this point, they would either drug me or want to cut something out. I was done with that path. I continued to get adjusted regularly. Adjustments helped break up the energetic stress patterns stuck in the body and kept the channels open, so the life force could do its job. In addition, for me, it was time to go within. The stress of failing the exam combined with the stress the relationship uncovered created havoc in my body. I knew this was emotional. The headaches seemed to change from daily to weekly. I was starting to begin to scratch the surface of connecting my thoughts, my emotions, and my state of mind with my physical state. During that last year of school, I was aware that I was not happy. I was about to graduate and found my purpose with chiropractic, but on a day-to-day basis, I began to question life without the haze of school to worry about. I felt inspiration adjusting people, but what else was going on? My relationship ended, and I had to say goodbye to my chiropractic cocoon. I graduated in December 1997. I was twenty-three years old. My real-life education was about to begin.

CHAPTER 4

OPENING MY PRACTICE

I went back to my hometown to open my own practice. It was a lesson on how small business is tortured by bureaucracy and nonsensical red tape. I opened on my own because I did not fully align with how other local chiropractors practiced. I adjusted the spine for specific subluxations to clear stress in the body for optimal life force flow, optimal function, and optimal well-being. I had an affordable cash practice. I did not take insurance because I did not want them to dictate how I practiced. I could not play their game of filling out forms for diagnosis and prognosis. I was not treating symptoms and playing medical doctor. Chiropractic was different. It was about empowering others to get in tune with their mind, body, and energy. I reminded people that they can heal and that sometimes it takes longer than expected.

As soon as I opened my office door on March 23, 1998, it was as if this spiritual world opened for me, and new awareness began. I remember looking at the four walls of my office, wondering if I would be stuck in that space for the rest of my life. It felt kind of small and confining. Now I had to get people into my office. I was already sharing with others how chiropractic changed my life. I then realized people might think I was only telling them to get adjusted so I could make money. I was horrified by that thought. Chiropractic was so sacred to me. I had a difficult time taking money for my adjustments in the beginning.

I was also a bit shocked when I found most people did not want to hear what I had to say. One woman I knew growing up was on the verge of going blind with an eye disease. Since she was someone I looked up to and wanted to help, I offered her complimentary adjustments. I told her that I had seen many case studies where people's vision improved with adjustments. I even learned of a small child whose eyes uncrossed after getting adjusted. I told her the adjustments were gentle and easy. Worst-case scenario, nothing happens. Best-case scenario, your eyes improve. She was afraid. *What?* I noticed that she had a terribly negative attitude about life in general. Why wouldn't she want to help herself? I found this extremely perplexing. Does such a negative mind-set contribute to the dis-ease of the body? I know it does. She never ever did let me adjust her in all my eighteen years of practice.

I saw this happen often, people choosing not to help themselves. It really bothered me, especially in the beginning. There was another friend who was a nurse, and she was going to get surgery for sciatic pain. I told her to put off the surgery and try getting adjusted. She declined. She said she was already scheduled for surgery and it was just easier. *What?* Another woman was going to her doctor for a menstrual issue. I told her do not let them cut anything out. Go find out their opinion and let us talk about it. She let them admit her to the hospital that same day for a hysterectomy. She told me she did not have time to deal with it. She just had to get rid of the problem. *What?* I walked around dumbfounded. I thought people were uninformed about healing, but I never knew they did not want to know. How many of us are walking around with suppressed immune systems from so many unnecessary drugs and surgeries?

I had one more experience with the medical world before I walked away for good. I had a topical cyst in my groin. It had been there for a while. I had them before as a teenager and had them medically cut out. This time I thought it was not healing because it was right where my underwear hit, being continually irritated. I decided to get it removed. It was a quick outpatient procedure at lunchtime, and I was able to go back to my office. Within a few hours, I felt a throbbing pressure in my groin. I went to the bathroom to look at my incision. I was horrified when I saw a golf ball–sized swelling growing beneath the bandage. I was more horrified at myself for playing the medical game. I called the doctor and ended up in the emergency room.

Another doctor looked at the mass and told me the original doctor hit a blood vessel, and I was bleeding. He told me I had to get stitches and would have to take antibiotics. *Ugh, here we go again with this crap.* I was lying there, so upset for having put myself in that situation. I told him I did not want antibiotics and asked if there was a way to let it heal naturally. This guy became flustered, telling me how dangerous it was if I did not take antibiotics. I lay there quietly, not saying a word, hating myself because I knew better than entering the medical world. I do not vibrate there anymore. Any belief I had left in the medical world was completely gone. The doctor began to ask me questions about my life, trying to start small talk, probably because I looked so upset. He asked me if I was in school or if I worked. I mumbled that I was a chiropractor. He asked if I was a chiropractic student. I told him, "No, I am a chiropractor." Suddenly, he changed his story. He told me we could let the incision stay open without stitches, if I would keep it clean, and I would not have to take the antibiotics. *What the hell.* I said, "Good, let us do that." I could not wait to get the hell out of there. I was finished with the medical world. That was twenty-two years ago, and I have never been back.

When I opened my office, I had an x-ray machine installed. The chiropractic technique that I practiced used x-ray as part of its protocol. After spending about $20,000 on this machine, I began to question using it within two months. I always went with what I felt with my hands regardless of the x-ray. The energy I began to feel working on each person was starting to overtake me, and I did not have words to describe it. I fought with myself that I did not know enough to stop using x-ray. Then I met another chiropractor, not too far from me, who did not x-ray. He used a light touch technique. It consisted of lightly touching the spine in certain areas to release the meningeal ligaments, which attach the spinal cord to the spine. I saw this technique in chiropractic school, but it looked like voodoo to me. I liked a specific adjustment where I felt or heard the bone crack. With this other technique, I would watch people lie on the table; the chiropractor barely touched them with his fingertips, and people would start releasing on the table. Releasing looked like deep breathing, crying, or wavelike motions. I never felt anything because I was so locked down emotionally and physically for so long. I was slowly coming alive.

The years in chiropractic school got me stabilized and out of pain. I was about to embark on a new level of awareness. I began getting adjusted by this chiropractor. I would lie on the table, and he would hold light pressure with his hand on my sacrum (the center triangular bone in my pelvis), then touch a few areas along my spine and maybe give me a structural or cracking adjustment in my neck. My low back started to wake me up at three o'clock every morning, feeling on fire, for about a year. An entire new layer of my spine and my being was coming alive. I became so sensitive to energy. I sold my x-ray machine after fighting with myself for nine months. I adjusted based solely on what I felt with my hands, including doing the light touch technique that I was learning every week. It helped me integrate all the energy I was feeling working on people.

I read even more books. I loved *Autobiography of a Yogi* by Paramahansa Yogananda. That book was incredible. He mentioned yogis who got so in tune with their energy that they could walk through walls, bilocate, and go without food. I subscribed to and studied his life and meditation lessons for three years. I began to be repulsed by meat, and I had to change my products to natural ones. I could not stand the chemical smell. Your body will tell you what it does or does not need if you listen to it.

During this time, I went to Brazil three years in a row on chiropractic mission trips. The first year was in September 1999 for ten days. There were twelve of us chiropractors. We went to the city of Fortaleza. My chiropractic friend from Tennessee adjusted a person in his office from that city. She organized everything and housed us in a large community center. We each set up our tables early in the morning, and people lined up in droves to get adjusted. We adjusted eight to ten hours a day for about five days. Most of the people spoke Portuguese, and we spoke English, so it was silent energy work done with our hands. It was magic. We would adjust one another at night. The energy was like none I had ever felt. We all sat around together after adjusting one another, feeling high, completely giddy, blissed out, and there were no drugs of any kind. That high stayed with me all week. When I got home, I crashed. I could not maintain that high vibe in my normal routine. I fell into a depressed state for about a month. My passion for chiropractic kept me going. I continued to read about spirituality and energy work. I discovered the poets Rumi and Hafiz and knew they had tapped into that same energy. I understood exactly what their poetry was saying.

I continued to read about other subjects too, business and money. I was building a practice without one ounce of education about those topics. The book that stopped me in my tracks was *Rich Dad Poor Dad* by Robert Kiyosaki. All the others seemed to be like blah, blah, blah until this one. The lightbulb went off for me, just like when I read the chiropractic philosophy for the first time. The author said that to become financially free, you must build assets that pay you residual income whether you work or not. If you are employed or self-employed, you will never be financially free, because you are trading time for money. He explained how we are following an old paradigm, where you go to college to get a good-paying job. Schools do not teach us to be financially free. *I knew it.* I was pissed. I knew I wasted my time in school.

Even with chiropractic school, the ones who just went through the regular classes ended up not being good chiropractors. It was all the extracurricular meetings and seminars that taught real chiropractic. I had many chiropractic colleagues who were either clueless about chiropractic or compromised their principles for money. I had a friend who went to my chiropractic college and graduated about a year after me. I offered for her to share space in my office. She covered for me when I went to Brazil. A new woman came to my office while I was away. My friend took the visit, but she never adjusted her. I guess she did a consultation. She told her to come back next week when I was there. She told me she did not know what to do with her because she was in a wheelchair. I said, "You palpate her spine and adjust any subluxations you feel!" I met the lady in the wheelchair. She was easy to adjust. However, she believed she was limited in her movement from having polio when she was young. She wanted me to only adjust her neck while sitting in the wheelchair. I wanted her to get on the table so I could check and adjust her entire spine. Oh, the possibilities of her body really healing, but she was afraid. I never got her on the table. I adjusted her neck for many years. People argue for their limitations. My friend ended up leaving my practice after a year. She never built anything. She could not even face me in person; she left me a voice mail. I saw she joined a chiropractic clinic where she probably did not have to know how to adjust. They did car accidents, worker's compensation, and insurance. Most just lay people on therapy beds, fill out insurance forms, and collect their money.

I had another friend who I met at chiropractic school. He decided to open a practice near my hometown about six months before I graduated. I was excited that I would have someone nearby who could adjust me. Once I was back and opened my practice, we would sometimes meet for lunch. I sensed something was changing. He hired a coach to help build his practice. A few months later, I covered his practice while he was on vacation. I was brokenhearted when I saw how he was practicing. He was using fear to get people to come regularly. His office was doing everything that would allow them to get paid by insurance. We were supposed to be lights in the world, not adding more fear. He built a "successful" practice. Today he lives a very wealthy lifestyle with homes, cars, and more. I do not know how he sleeps at night. I've seen what money and lack of money does to people.

Rich Dad Poor Dad blew my mind in so many ways. When I was about seven, my grandfather opened another store at age seventy-nine because he retired from his original shop and he was bored. He recruited my mom to work there part-time. I would go with her. I wanted to work too. I wanted to be a part of the group. I began cleaning shelves every week for five dollars. One day, out shopping with my mom, I saw a pretty little red pocketbook with navy straps and red strawberries on the trim. It was twenty dollars. My mom told me to save my money. I did. It took me one month. I was so excited to buy my little red pocketbook. That excitement lasted about a week, and then I did not care about the pocketbook. I also felt the angst that it took me a month to earn the money for something that thrilled me for about a week.

I experienced the same angst when I bought my first car. Three years of working at a job I dreaded to get this car that kept costing me money. How many hours a week was I working to pay for car expenses? It happened again when I opened my practice. *How many people do I have to adjust to pay for my rent, my car, my utilities, my business licenses, insurance, and so on?* This is insane. Not one person in my life ever discussed this Rich Dad way of thinking. He said the rich think and speak differently than the poor and middle class. I was surrounded by middle-class and poor thinking. I related this concept to health. Once I understood health, I spoke differently. I did not want people to call me Dr. Lynn in my office; they called me Lynn. I wanted them to know that they were their own best doctor. I did not use the term *patients* for the people in my practice. They were not sick. They were well. I still will not use the phrase "I'm sick" for myself. I will say, "My body is expressing symptoms," "I'm out of balance," or "I need to rest."

According to Rich Dad, poor people say, "I can't afford that," and rich people say, "How can I afford that?" I noticed how beliefs and programming shape your health, your wealth, and everything else in your life. I learned to mind my mind, my thoughts, and my words. I can tell when I speak to someone where their consciousness is by the words they speak to me. I called out a friend when I heard her say, "I'm broke." She got angry and adamantly declared to me, "But I am broke." *Wow,* I thought. *Why do we declare our limitations?* All that working hard in school, and more than ten years of working part-time while in school, all for nothing. So much striving and struggle, along with too much medical intervention, made me sick and depressed.

Why are there so many struggling people out there? Our system sets them up for it. Then they are so programmed they argue for their limitations. This is the rat race. I freed myself from the limited thinking about my health, and now I was on a mission to make myself financially free. I did not know how yet, but I was going to figure it out. I began asking people around me about these asset-building concepts. No one had a clue. Still to the present day, I mention the *Rich Dad* book in conversation, and I wait for the other person's reaction. Either they've never heard of it, or they said they've read it. I can tell, the more we talk, if they really understand the concept. Most people do not get it. How can you not be completely woken up understanding the concept of residual income? There is a quote by Art Jonak, "If you understood residual income, you would walk through a brick wall to get it." What would your life look like if you had residual (reoccurring) income every month to cover your living expenses and your preferred lifestyle?

I went to India in October 2000 for a mission trip and a wedding. Another chiropractor friend had grandparents who lived in Calcutta. He wanted to not only have an Indian wedding but also adjust people in the homes established by Mother Teresa. That trip was filled with mixed experiences and emotions. I was not prepared for the harshness of the environment. I could not breathe because the pollution was extremely thick. I felt as if my face was behind an exhaust pipe. There was filth everywhere. People, animals, cars, and noise were crowding me at every turn. We were being driven in an old white minivan when two other cars crashed into both sides of us. All the drivers, including ours, kept driving without blinking an eye. It was crazy. Henna ink was painted on my hands for the wedding. My hands smelled so badly afterward; I could not put them near my face when I slept. The wedding was quite an event. I wore a beautiful red sari. The groom rode in on a white horse. The colors, music, and food were amazing. I freaked out seeing a few huge black rats running around.

The next day we went to Mother Teresa's home to adjust the nuns. I stood by Mother Teresa's marble white tomb. The energy was so powerful. It overtook me and made me cry. Each day, we went to different homes set up for the poor. I adjusted in an orphanage, where all the little babies in cribs were lined up in this huge room. My heart broke. I wanted to take them all home with me. It was too much. I adjusted in the home for the dying, beds lined up in another large room, with people ready to die. We split up, and some of the chiropractors went to the home of the lepers. These people were still considered outcasts.

I had many realizations on this trip. What we focus on grows. When we start something, do we want to perpetuate it or change it? I connected how the medical world focuses on disease and seems to create more and more disease. Similarly, I connected that by naming a huge building "The Home for the Dying," you must keep filling it with dying people. How about naming it, "The Home for the Living"? I wanted to empower others, not keep them in need. In Brazil, I felt so much soul-connected living; it made me hate the American materialistic culture. However, the filth and chaos in India made me appreciate our materialistic culture. There must be a balance between these two extremes.

Last, I could not wear my contact lenses in India with all the pollution. They would dry up in my eyes, and I had to take them out. I never traveled with glasses, so my eyes had to get used to being free. I had read a book, *Take Off Your Glasses and See* by Dr. Jacob Liberman. He explained how our eyes see using the entire periphery, not by focusing on one small area. Glasses and contact lenses make you focus only on the center, losing the periphery. This weakens the eye muscles. I had tried going without lenses prior to India. However, I panicked with my blurry vision and put the lenses immediately back in. In India, I had no choice but to go around with blurry vision. Then I began to see! It took maybe a few hours to a day for me to trust that my eyes were already getting stronger. That was twenty years ago, and I still do not wear lenses. I do not have any problem seeing. I cannot imagine how weak my eyes would be had I continued to wear lenses all these years.

My next trip to Brazil was September 2000. It was magical and empowering, but it was my third trip, in September 2001, that changed my life. We did not just stay inside the community centers to adjust people; we went out to the streets in the middle of the city. I did not find my high; I found my low. I got bug bites all over my face. We were supposed to fly home on September 11, 2001, but American Airlines somehow mixed up our flights. We had to fly home the day before. I did not fight it because I felt like shit. I had a fever, felt nauseas, and felt like I was going to die. Another chiropractor told me I was burning off everything I energetically, emotionally, and physically did not need. I was hoping they let me on the plane because I looked awful. It was the longest thirteen-hour flight of my life. I arrived home late that night, only to wake up to my haze of symptoms and the horrific events of 911. It took me a week to recover from the bug bites, the fever, and the queasiness.

I know the world has a lot of names for bug bites, but I did not go to the medical doctor to get a diagnosis. I had enough of that. The physical symptoms left after a week, but what lingered was an energetic darkness. There was sadness and mourning all over the country from the attacks in New York City, but this was different. I did not know how else to describe it, except that I was walking in a cloud of murkiness. It lingered for the next six weeks. A woman, who I adjusted regularly in my office, told me that I was carrying a lot of dark energy. I never mentioned it to her. She revealed she does shamanic healings. She worked with spirit guides. She recommended soaking in Epsom salt baths for a week, lighting a white candle, and telling the darkness to go to the light. I did this for a week, and the murkiness I felt lifted. I was flying high. And this time, the flying high did not leave. I was blissed out, and it lasted for eighteen months.

I began having shamanic healing sessions with the woman for about a year. I never took anything internally. She did energy work on me followed by a message from her guides. Every few months, I felt my bliss vibe getting deeper. Any problems that I thought I had dissolved into nothing. I seriously loved everyone, and most people got on my nerves. I stopped going out drinking with my friends. I was already high. I could just sit with myself and do nothing. Any physical symptoms I may have had regularly, including headaches and menstrual problems, were gone. I began reading the stories of saints and people who had near-death experiences and saw the light. They described my experience exactly; otherwise, there were no words. I laughed, remembering friends discussing how it could or could not be possible for a Catholic to marry someone Jewish. I figured it out. Jesus was just showing us the power we had. Half the people began worshipping him, and the other half killed him because he was blasphemous. The governmental authorities had to silence him. They could not have their programmed slaves wake up. I do not think Jesus wanted any of it. He wanted to show us all what we could do. We are made in the image and likeness of God. God or Source is within us.

Anyone who has tapped into this energetic space could never define themselves with any religious label. This is the space where miraculous healings occur. This is who we are when we leave the physical body. Once we clear the programming, we can tap into this energy here in our physical bodies. We are pure consciousness. We have the power. This power is our natural state. We just do not believe it. We have been numbed down by societal rules, government, schooling, medicine, and religions. I was free. The underlying restlessness that festered within me disappeared, and I was filled with grace.

Once the blinders came off, I was never the same. I saw through other healers. I could tell who experienced this state or not, by their words and actions. For instance, one healer I knew was constantly *working* on herself. I told her I did not need healing sessions anymore. I did not need to heal anything; I was healed. I stopped getting adjusted. I had been trying to find someone to adjust me, but most other chiropractors' energy was a lower frequency than mine. I was better clearing myself with my mind.

At this point, I had been doing yoga for about five years. One day after finishing a class, I began laughing. So much struggle to find spirituality when it is who we are. I was already doing yoga every minute of my life. I stopped having a strict routine and only did the exercise, yoga, if I was inspired to. In fact, I only did anything if I felt inspired. I was healed, whole, mindful, and fully present. I had an out-of-body reset with how I ate too. I became fully detached from my food. I did not judge it anymore. I intuitively knew in the moment if something would agree with my body. Until this present day, I usually choose clean meals and crave healthy foods, but sometimes I must eat heavy toxic food, like fast food, because it helps ground me. I get so high in vibration that I cannot ground myself to perform daily activities. I ate less at each meal. I could not overeat if I wanted, because the discomfort was terrible. It would wreck my energy. I was never needing to lose weight, but about ten pounds dissipated and never came back, even after seventeen years and a pregnancy. It was true alignment. At this point, some part of me left wanting to practice chiropractic. What once felt like inside-out healing now felt like outside in. Every person who came to me to get adjusted I knew was already healed; they just did not believe it. It is the truth. Disease is only around today because of our beliefs.

Over the eighteen years of adjusting people in my practice, I came to understand how stress affects the life force flowing through the body. Think of the life force (energy) flowing through the brain, spinal cord, nerves, and out to every organ, and then back from every organ, to the nerves, spinal cord, and brain, communicating with one another. It is like a hose conducting water from the spout to the garden. If you step on the hose, the flow of water will decrease or stop until you take your foot off the hose. This happens to our life force. As a chiropractor, I checked the spine to feel for motion of each spinal joint; lack of motion and swollen tissue around it indicated a subluxation. Subluxation means pressure on the nerve and interference of the life force flowing through that area of the spine. I adjusted the joint to clear the interference, to create better flow, better communication, and better function.

Chronic stress led to chronic stress patterns and sometimes chronic symptoms. Some common stresses were not enough time, not enough money, worrying about money, making ends meet with money every month, working at a job they hated, feeling no passion or purpose in life, worrying about taking care of children emotionally and financially, relationships, feeling trapped with no way out of the rat race, not enough money or time to choose alternative health treatments or buy organic foods and clean products. Living this way causes stress, decreases energy flow, and creates dis-ease and eventually disease. I had to connect the dots for people that their mental stresses were coming out physically in the body. I was amazed at how many people did not understand that.

We are so programmed that disease is something we catch outside ourselves, just like we are programmed that healing happens outside ourselves with every pill we take. Let me break it down: disease and healing are an inside job. It starts with the thoughts we think, the beliefs that hold us hostage, and the lifestyle we choose to live. I can adjust someone all day long, but if he or she continues to lead an unfulfilled, unhappy, and stressed life, he or she will not have well-being. What are you giving your energy to every day? It is okay to do something temporarily if you have a plan B that excites you. Do you have purpose? I see so many people working at dead-end jobs, working hard for other people, and never building anything for themselves. What happens if you lose that job? What happens when you make that sale? Unless it is creating residual income, you will always have to make another sale. How long can you trade time for money? Do you have the option of taking time off, if you or your loved one needs to heal, and still get paid? I am amazed at the amount of people never addressing these issues. I believe this is one of the complex array of reasons people get disease. If they do not face these issues, disease can be a subconscious way out. I remember being in the hospital thinking it was better than my life. What relationships are draining you? It takes courage to face these issues, but if you do not, you will not have well-being.

I knew a woman who was amazing. She battled with cancer for a long time. She really took the time to get alternative treatments. She came to me for adjustments, went to the acupuncturist I recommended, read healing books, cleaned up her diet, and took supplements. She was genuinely evolving as a person. However, she still went for chemotherapy and radiation, which I wish she had stopped. Most of all, she did not walk away from her alcoholic husband of forty-plus years. She depended on him for money. She had an extraordinarily strong Catholic family who did not believe in divorce. I know her fears, beliefs, and toxic relationship contributed to her cancer. She died more than ten years ago; her widowed husband is still drunk today. I do not think death is a bad thing. Maybe she could not evolve anymore in this lifetime and was ready for the next reality. I know we all are eternal consciousness. I believe we are here to find our eternalness in this body. I find so many people are afraid to die, and many live a long quantity in years, but they never fully live. Death is a grace.

I found it shocking that even alternative therapy healers still fear disease. I was at an event with other healers touring a hospital of all places. I heard someone say, "Oh I can get my mammogram here. Nice facility." See, I would never take a test like that. It is not necessary. Finding this state of true knowing is a journey, and we have been riddled with lies and fears for most of our lives. But it is possible to find. I never told people when to come to see me to get adjusted. In the first visit, depending on how much stress I felt in their body, I would recommend coming again the next week. I would take it visit to visit, and then I would tell them to decide when they wanted to come. You know when you feel you need it. I know I lost some people like that because they were programmed to be told what was wrong with them and given a treatment protocol. I cannot play that game.

One lady saw me a few times. She had a negative mind-set and was looking for someone to tell her what was wrong with her. I do not remember her exact symptoms, but I tried to comfort her that she would get better and it takes time. About a week later, I got a call from another chiropractor asking me for her records. This was not my finest moment, as I yelled at the other chiropractor. I asked him how he calls himself a chiropractor when he needed records. Stop playing medical doctor and stop playing into the fear drama. I never kept records. I only marked the date of the visit on people's cards. I charged twenty dollars a visit (raised it to twenty-five dollars after ten years), and people could take a receipt if they wished. I did not submit to insurance companies. If a lawyer called me to get records for a car accident, I told them I did not keep records. I only had the date of each visit, which I would give him. Did he want all the visits prior to the accident too? He hung up and never bothered me anymore. I have been asked if I would testify in court that a car accident can cause spinal pain. I said only if I could also state everything else that could cause spinal pain. I never heard back from them either. I want to see people doing things to change their lives. I gave them books, information, and suggestions all the time. I never got into practice for people to use me as a crutch. I wanted to empower others.

I am humbled and honored by all those who chose me as their chiropractor. I adjusted some amazing people. I especially cherished the kids that I adjusted. Quite a few I adjusted from birth, toddler, or young child through their high school or college graduation. I did not like watching them enter the rat race. I recommended *Rich Dad Poor Dad* so many times. I wanted to do more. I did help some make it through childhood with less medical intervention. It really upset me when I would see a child get ear tubes or a tonsillectomy, then be just as sick with colds, allergies, and sore throats afterward. I had a girl around age twelve come in after school. Her mother told me how the teacher said she had a bad day at school because she did not take her antihyperactivity medicine. I knew the mind-set of the mother; they were really entrenched in the medical world. I felt sick to my stomach that she thought it was funny that she had to give her child drugs to get through school. I felt like I was allowing child abuse. It is not your child who needs the drugs; she is the sane one. She is bursting with creativity and life, and you are trying to dumb her down for our broken, dysfunctional school system that does not help you at all in the real world. I was looking for a bigger platform to reach people. Playing chiropractor had become too mainstream for me. I was expanding too much.

CHAPTER 5

FIGURING OUT FINANCIAL FREEDOM

O nce I had my inner grace experience, the healing world became mundane. I did not need to figure out anything about health. Now I wanted my daily life to have the freedom I felt in the grace state. I knew I was not free being tied to my chiropractic office, and I knew the rat race was the main culprit why so many people were struggling with health issues. I was ready to figure this out. I continued to read everything I could about financial freedom. At least in chiropractic school, I was blessed to be in a cocoon of people working toward health freedom. Having mentors and like-minded people around me made these changes much easier. I could not find anyone who was working toward financial freedom. I did not realize at the time how spiritual money is. I also was not fully aware of the poverty consciousness that I carried. Just like my healing process was long and drawn out, so has been my financial journey. Here is a big tip: stay with the process whatever roadblocks you encounter along the way. The most excitement, bliss, wisdom, and empowerment come from moving through the roadblocks.

Rich Dad was all about changing your mind-set. He made his cashflow through starting businesses and holding rental real estate. He talked about learning to invest in stocks, but not by giving your money to a broker for them to diversify and invest in the long term. I never felt good about giving my power to a broker either. I wanted to understand more and did not know how. Regarding starting a business, I could not have imagined starting with an idea from nothing, where you eventually take it to the stock market and offer an IPO (initial public offering). He said this could create many jobs for people. I never wanted to create jobs for people. I wanted everyone to be financially free. Rich Dad mentioned network marketing as another option, but I had no understanding of that. I understood owning real estate and renting it out, so that was where I started.

There were a couple of reasons I started with real estate. First, I knew I could buy a building, put my office in it, and rent out the rest. Second, I had one older cousin on my dad's side. Together we inherited a piece of land from our grandparents. He was desperate to sell it because he never got out of the rat race and needed help upon his pending retirement. I was not ready to sell because I did not have a plan. He drove me crazy coming into my office weekly talking about this. I learned from my books that I would have to pay a big chunk on capital gains tax unless I rolled it into a property that I did not personally use for at least a few years through a tax exchange law. I took part of the money from the sale, paid a smaller tax, and put it as a down payment on a building. I could move my practice into it and rent the rest. My five-year lease was up on my office space anyway, so that became perfect timing. I decided to put the rest of the money in a duplex at the Jersey Shore to rent out. I grew up going to the shore every summer, and most people I knew always vacationed there. The town I picked was a place people lived in all year. I always saw property values go up, especially by the ocean.

At settlement for the land, my cousin was watching all the extra papers I was filling out, looking confused. I told him I was trying to protect myself from the capital gains tax. He looked alarmed. "What capital gains tax?" I was thinking, *How do you not know? You are almost sixty years old.* I was so tired of being surrounded by people so clueless about money. At the settlement for my office building, the monthly mortgage payment ended up being $500 more than what I thought the estimate was. I went through something similar when I opened my office and took out a loan against money my mom saved for me as collateral. The loan ended up being as much as my monthly rent. I realized the bankers I was working with were not financially free themselves and only doing what would benefit the bank. It was eye-opening for me realizing that the people who worked at the bank did not actually understand economics.

The building I bought for my office was old and had to be renovated. I had never done anything like that before, so I learned as I went. I spent many nights and weekends visiting Home Depot and working with many different handymen and contractors. It was overwhelming. The old lady who owned the building prior to me was a slum lord. The building had two apartments and one huge office space. The office was easy to divide into two units. The wall and doors were already there; I just closed both doors, and it was divided equally. I took one half for my office and rented the other half. One apartment had a tenant. I was painting my office space when my now tenant came over to see me to ask if he could have a stove. *What? There is not a stove in your apartment?* I went through inspection; how did I miss that? I must have been so overwhelmed, I assumed I saw a stove in the kitchen. Next thing I know, I was buying a special-sized stove to fit a special-sized kitchen. The adventures of owning properties continued to escalate for the next eleven years.

I finally found someone, a friend of a friend, who got the financial freedom concept, after looking for someone to learn with for a few years. We split the cost of real estate investing courses. We put $14,000 on a credit card. Rich Dad said the wealthy spend money on financial education and personal development. I was way out of my comfort zone doing this. It was a huge leap of faith for me. We took the courses, and I proceeded to buy two more properties. One was offered to us as a new construction deal through the real estate courses. I went in on the deal with the guy who I split the tuition with and another friend. They put the money up, and I signed for it. We planned to sell it in eighteen months. Next, I took $13,000 out in equity from the Jersey Shore property and bought a tiny townhouse that gave me two hundred dollars a month in positive cashflow. My one issue all the time was keeping cash flow because there was always an issue with a tenant or a repair. Even the taxes in New Jersey went up almost $800 a year. How does the average person pay that? In Delaware, the property taxes were cheaper. I did not know crossing the border ten minutes away could make such a difference. The real estate courses recommended budgeting for vacancy and maintenance. I found that impossible to budget. I find it interesting because my whole life, I always had the feeling of not enough money, even when I did. Going through this process really helped begin to clear those feelings. I was proud of what I had accomplished so far with my side hustle real estate ventures as I continued to practice chiropractic in my office.

CHAPTER 6

PERSONAL TRANSFORMATIONS

All this time, I was still living with my mom. I never could get a vision of what having my own life looked like. This was a big part of where my issues lied. When I was leaving college, I remember hearing friends decide where they wanted to live and practice. Some were getting married. I was twenty-three. I had never seen myself married. I thought I should go back to my hometown to be near my family. My mom was not home much because she always worked two jobs. It was quite simple to move back home upon opening my practice at first, but then I did not know how to move out. I felt so guilty leaving my mom alone. My mom had traditional beliefs where you move out when you get married. I had no plans to get married. By the time I was thirty and had my awakening, I knew I did not want to be married. I had no need to do it for religious reasons. I wanted to be financially independent. Marriage never really made sense to me. I never needed a legal document telling me I was tied to one person. I could decide that for myself.

Another factor that influenced me was the Rich Dad philosophy. Rich Dad did not consider owning your own home an asset. He said that was middle-class and poor thinking, so I felt stuck. I was not going out drinking like I used to, nor was I traveling as much. Once I felt the grace, I was just peaceful. After my real estate ventures were more established, I decided the one thing that moved my spirit was salsa dancing. I was introduced to Latin music in chiropractic school. I attended a few Latin music concerts and loved them, even though I do not remember getting home from the out-of-control drinking. I had many nights like that, getting so drunk and waking up with horrible hangovers. Many think it is normal for college kids to drink and party. I think it is a symptom of a destructive system in place. I felt like a caged animal, and when I drank, it helped me let go. I wondered what people did with their lives if they were not working during the week or partying on the weekends. That is part of the rat race mentality. I kept trying to see through the limitations of my mind. Every time I heard Latin music, something came alive within me. I thought I should follow that impulse.

I signed up for salsa lessons after searching for a bit; it was a process finding good lessons in Delaware. I took some bad group lessons, then eventually found a great instructor and took some private ones. I found the better salsa dancing happened thirty miles north of where I lived in Philadelphia. One night at a club in Philly, I danced with someone, and I felt a spiritual connection. My friend who I was with was making me leave early, but I told her to wait because I wanted to give this guy my number. She wrote my number on a napkin, went over to the guy, said, "My friend wants you to call her," stuffed the napkin with my number in his pocket, and we quickly left. Talk about getting things done!

In all the relationships I had, I usually was unattached unless the person left me. I think when they left, it would trigger the grief and abandonment issues I had from my dad's death. I also was attached to the high of when you are falling in love or the high of that chemical attraction. Now I was coming from a completely different vibe. I knew that high vibe was within me. I was great by myself and not attached to an outcome. He called me. He had moved from a Latin country only a few years prior. I loved his accent. His English was new, but I could understand everything he said perfectly. It had to be a past-life soul connection because we fell into being together rather quickly. Within a few weeks, we were fighting like crazy people too. We had so much passion and chemistry. I knew if I wanted dating privacy, I needed to get out of my mom's house. Within four months, I moved into an apartment with him. Next thing I knew, I was pregnant. I was scared to death. This was way too permanent a situation to commit to. He was so happy. I was terrified and did not know if I should keep it.

At this point in my life, I knew to follow my gut. I was thirty-one years old; maybe this was meant to be. So many people try to get pregnant, and I did not even try. I think others thought I was at that age where I was afraid of not finding someone and having a baby. That could not have been further from the truth. It really was a natural, organic unfolding of me following my inner guidance. I walked around during the months I was pregnant in a dumbfounded state, borderline depressed. My heart felt like I was supposed to be doing this, but my mind was screaming no. I knew two women who did not like being moms, and I saw lots of people who had no business being a parent. What if I did not take to it? I could not give it back. I was not sure if I wanted kids or if I should be bringing kids into this world.

I had another lady I adjusted who was a trained counselor, and she read tarot cards. I went to see her. She told me that this unborn soul and I had made an agreement to come together at this time. That explained the feeling that I should be doing this. What about the darkness that I felt? Was I harming the baby? She told me no, because I was working out my own stuff and clearing the way for things to unfold. I resonated with that, and I trusted her. I will be forever grateful to this woman who was a great light during this time.

I had no physical symptoms during my pregnancy, only the depression I felt. I gained only twenty pounds. Physically, I was perfectly healthy, but it was the first time I felt out of control and vulnerable with something else inhabiting my body. I decided I better search out someone to regularly adjust me. I knew the adjustments would help me energetically work through the experience and ground me. I knew the midwife I wanted. I had worked with her when I first opened my practice, helping her with state licensing issues and fighting the vaccine world. Being pregnant was the first time I felt vulnerable and exposed. Now other people would have to know about my personal life. My belly would grow. I would be subjected to their questions and comments. I still did not want to get married, not even a bit. It was the first time I was exposing all of myself, and it was hard.

Another part of my old programming lingered. I felt uncomfortable having a child while living in an apartment. I kept thinking that in Delaware, it was cheaper to have a mortgage than pay rent. I saw a house for sale down the street from my office, in the neighborhood I grew up in. It was a great neighborhood for first-time home buyers. I went to the guy at Countrywide, who did many of my mortgages, to ask how much I would need to put down on the property. I thought I could eventually refinance some of my properties or sell one. He barely took a breath to tell me he could get me financed for the entire $200,000. This was March 2006, and it was Countrywide; most of us know how this story will play out. I thought, *Take the deal, get the house, have the baby in June, and then you can figure out how to reorganize your monies and equities.* I had settlement in May 2006 and moved in immediately. Life was moving at full speed ahead.

I finished adjusting clients in my office the evening of June 13. I did not realize how much I physically used my core to adjust people until I had a huge pregnant belly. I went home and eventually went to bed for the night. Around three o'clock, I woke up feeling weird. Was I in labor? I had no idea when or how it would happen, which is such a strange thing. I called my midwife and told her what I was feeling. She said to go back to sleep and call her in the morning. I slept on and off and immediately called her. She came over to check me and stayed for a while, setting things up. By that evening, I was still having sporadic pains, but not much else was changing. The two grandmothers came to be a part of the birth. This was the first grandchild for both. My partner still had to go to work. The moms followed me around my house as I paced through intermittent labor pains for three days.

The last twenty-four hours were the most intense. We were up all night, including my midwife and her two assistants. There was a birthing pool set up. I was in and out of that. It did not help. My midwife gave me wine to help relax; it would not go down. I kept wanting to sit on the toilet. That was where I found relief. I realized that the five years of having my menstrual episodes were just like labor. I knew how to go within myself until the next pain passed. Lying on my back was the most excruciating pain, even if I was propped up. Most commonly, I see pictures of women in the hospital, giving birth, lying on their backs in the bed. No wonder they need drugs or end up with a cesarean section. I needed to walk around. Eventually, I found my comfortable position in the birthing chair. One of the midwives asked me if there was anything holding me back mentally from giving birth. I answered, "Yes!" I still did not believe that a baby was coming out. Then she gave me a smelling oil, and it started happening. I was truly in the zone on the birthing chair until my midwife asked me if I wanted to see the baby's head crowning. I came out of my zone for a second, looked with a hand mirror, and panicked. The opening did not look big enough to allow a baby to come through. As soon as I had that panic thought, my body contracted, and out my son came, tearing me. If I had not looked, it would have been so much better.

My midwife put me on the nearby bed and laid my son on my chest. She let him lay there until the umbilical cord stopped pulsing and the afterbirth came out. Then she stitched and cleaned me up and cleaned the baby. He latched on to nurse immediately. He was perfect. It was Friday, June 16, 2006, at 2:44 p.m. We named him Gilfredo Roberto because it was a family name. I just liked the name because it was unique and felt powerful. Eight pounds, eight ounces, tons of dark hair, and he looked like a replica of my baby pictures. I never even thought he could look like me. I remember him crying while my midwife was sewing up the cord. I grabbed his little hand and thought, *I got you. I will always protect you.* No drugs, no circumcision, no vaccines, no interference, and he was beautiful! I checked his spine, and it was clear.

I could not have had better care or a more magical birth

experience, thanks to my midwives. They massaged my back, eased my mind, and allowed me to have my own unique experience. They moved divinely like angels. I barely knew they were there yet felt immense support. They knew how to hold the energy. It only cost $3,000 for the all the pregnancy checkups and the entire birth process. I paid it myself. I got rid of health insurance in 1999 when I finally decided that I am not investing in disease for my future. I know this may shock a lot of people, but when you know, you know. I am shocked to find people who keep a job for benefits. Talk about having no power over yourself.

My midwife had been in practice for more than thirty years and had eight children herself. The older ones were vaccinated, including her older son, who was also circumcised. The middle ones had half the vaccines; the more she learned, she changed her beliefs. Her younger ones were not vaccinated at all, including her younger son not being circumcised. She has fought for her right to practice, including the rights for women to choose where they give birth. We all owe women like this immense gratitude. Why should we have someone tell us where we can give birth? I find it strange that women give birth in hospitals where it houses so much sickness and disease. Many think this is normal to bring new life into that kind of environment. I think it is crazy.

The first six weeks were a bit intense. My baby was fussy, and I was coming unglued. I had too many visitors and activities, and the stress of everything happening was too much on my relationship. I went back to practice after only three weeks, even though my midwife begged me to take off for six. I was worried about the bills and keeping my practice closed that long. I did have the same woman who adjusted me during my pregnancy hold office hours for me a few times. Someone gave me the book *The Baby Whisperer*, and that really helped figure out my son's rhythms of nursing, playing, bathing, and sleeping. After six weeks, as the fog lifted a bit, I realized I should have listened to my midwife. I was trying to find my new normal too quickly and could not pull it together. I was not on my game like before. I was looking for my grace state, but I could not seem to find it. The grace was all coming from my baby; once he found his routine, he was so easy and so happy. I did not know it yet, but the core issues of my entire life were about to become clear as I moved through this darkness.

I was also questioning all the patterns showing up for myself and in my relationship. When you begin to question your normal, it can be a challenge to see the invisible web that binds you. I discovered the book *Codependent No More* by Melody Beattie, and it connected so many dots. In my own words, this book said that the alcoholic, the caretaker, and the workaholic have all the same codependent patterns. *That was it.* I had so many lights come on and was clearly understanding so many dynamics. Once I could see it, I could start to move toward shifting these patterns. I saw I had these same patterns as a caretaker, wanting to change the world through chiropractic and especially feeling guilty for taking money for my services. I was a workaholic. I struggled with bringing money in and felt guilty spending time for enjoyment. It felt frivolous for me to spend on something I did not consider a necessity; it would cause me to self-sabotage and block out abundance. All the times I was out partying and got drunk helped me let go and escape the stress of my daily life. I have so much gratitude for all the experiences I had during this time because it brought to light so many patterns I had in my life and helped me uncover these core issues about myself that I couldn't seem to grasp. Eventually, my relationship dissolved, but I had come out feeling so whole, grateful for everything it had shown me.

Then there was my son. I could see for the first time how life was supposed to be through him. I had felt the grace state but was trying to integrate it into my material world. I could feel how pure, happy, peaceful, and abundant my son naturally was, and how it is always there unless interfered with. My job as a mom was to protect his voice and protect his alignment to his inner guidance. My soul was blossoming from having this soul join my life. He nursed for a year. He ate a lot. In fact, I began looking like I had an eating disorder. You could see the muscle striations in my thighs, and my clothes were hanging on me. I may have been a size four, but now I had to buy a size zero. I ate everything I could because my son nursed it all out of me. I used to be 125 pounds before I had my grace state, which brought me down to 115 pounds. Now I was one hundred pounds, and my son weighed twenty-five pounds. My original weight now consisted of two people. He slept like clockwork, 8:00 p.m. to 8:00 a.m. every day with a two-hour nap in midafternoon. He started organic baby food at six months. I only brought him to a pediatrician to get the birth certificate signed since the state did not accept my midwife's signature.

She recommended a doctor she knew would not bother me about vaccines. I went to this doctor, and he told me how perfect my child was and that he only recommended one vaccine. He further explained why he recommended it. I got my certificate signed and got the hell out of there. I did not need his expertise to tell me my baby was perfect, and if he really understood the healing dynamic of the body, he would not be recommending that one vaccine either. I was so glad that I went through my own healing journey, including my cocoon years of the chiropractic world, so I could easily make decisions for my son. I really feel compassion for mothers who are starting to wake up once they are pregnant, or once they have their child, because they really have no support to make these decisions except the tyrannical medical world that is filled with a paradigm of fears. It takes work to find your own way and to find the right information and support. Plus, you are not in your right mind after having a baby. You are healing from giving birth and learning how to have another human in your life who needs you for everything. I was also blessed to be able to have part-time office hours without a pay cut, and my mom could watch him while I adjusted. I was still working on becoming financially free. I wanted income coming in to pay all my bills whether I worked or not. It felt more important than ever, now having my son.

I never restricted foods from my son. If someone gave him a lollipop or candy while we were out, I let him have it. I was not going to prohibit him from things he wanted to eat at home and then have him go to a friend's house to gorge himself on junk food. Our bodies are bigger than the food we eat if we can find that flow for ourselves. Most of us have not been allowed to just be with food, especially when we get into our social culture of judging and labeling everything. My son stopped nursing, himself, at eleven months. He always loved meat. I preferred fish and vegetables. He did not lean toward healthy or junk foods. He had an eclectic palette from the beginning. He liked spicy food and unique combos. I am not a cook, so this continues to be a delicate daily juggle. I never had one issue with allowing him to eat whatever he wanted. He had to learn himself what agrees with his system. He never was hyper if he had a soda. I think when parents say that, there is more going on in that scenario. The parent does not have themselves figured out and now is trying to control the child. My advice: stay out of your child's way. He or she has their own guidance system. You learn to follow yours and allow your child to follow theirs. They are here to teach us anyway, not the other way around. I had to undo everything that had been taught to me. I knew as a child the stuff I am relearning today; if only I had been allowed to follow my own guidance system. My son reminds me how wonderful life is daily. I always nurture what he shows interest in.

At three and a half, I gave him private art lessons. A wonderful woman, whom I adjusted, was an artist and a schoolteacher. She allowed him to explore and create whatever art inspired him every week. He took lessons from her for seven years. She even let him share his feelings, and she helped him understand his emotions while doing his art. Talk about art therapy! He began jiujitsu lessons at three and a half at his dad's suggestion. He loved that too. He took that for more than six years until he earned his green belt, which, we were disappointed to learn, was the highest you can go until you are sixteen. We would watch his favorite movies over and over. We watched so many awesome ones, but I especially remember watching *Cars* for six months straight and the *Curious George* movie. I loved it. I cherish every minute with my son. It has been a magical ride.

We began going to Barnes and Noble because they had a *Thomas the Train* table set up that he loved. He would play there for hours, and I would get my coffee and a book and chill. Those Barnes and Noble trips turned into a weekly mall day once a new one opened, attached to our mall. I remember seeing a new Lego store at the mall, not believing that could be its own store. Little did I know that I was about to become its best customer. As my son outgrew Thomas, we went into the Lego store and discovered a whole new magical world. I never knew how cool Lego sets had become. Wednesday afternoons became our mall day. I would close my office at one, and we would head to the mall. We both looked forward to it. We had lunch in the food court, Gilfredo picked out a Lego, and we headed to the Barnes and Noble café. He built his Lego while I enjoyed a coffee and a book or a magazine. We walked around the mall, did whatever shopping needed to be done that week, including Target, and then headed to jiujitsu class by 6:00 p.m. It was the best. We did this for years.

At first, I felt my lack issues buying a Lego set every week. I would never have done that for myself, but seeing through my son's eyes, I felt abundance and saw no problem with it. I watched my words very carefully when discussing money with my son. I did not want to pass on the lack mind-set to him. I was still working through my own money issues. I never told him we could not afford something. I would say, "Okay, you want that. Let us plan for it." He was always happy with that answer. And we did plan. It gave me a chance to find alignment with the purchase, and the finances would fall into place. Gilfredo continues to do this for himself today. I am always amazed how abundant he is and how he continually lines up with the money he desires. I had others accuse me of spoiling Gilfredo. For the first time, spending money on fun felt like inspired abundance. I felt wealth with my son. I was on a journey to become financially free when I got pregnant, and I could not figure out how that manifestation matched that intent. Now I understood in a big way. I was looking for the freedom in feeling abundant and having choices in my life in every moment. My son was showing me this. It was the first time I could really grasp it within the material world. Our mall days were transforming for me. And so much fun! Actually, every day was and is fun with my son. I hear people say that they cannot wait for their kids to go back to school. I never wanted to be away from my son. He was always so peaceful and joyful to be around.

I knew I was not sending him to school. I would not put him through that nightmare. I still have not recovered from the trauma. I feel it is such a waste of time. I did not know what homeschooling looked like, but I was going to figure it out. I learned about homeschooling when I went to chiropractic school with other students whose parents were chiropractors. They were raised without drugs and were homeschooled. I asked the state if they had a curriculum I could follow; they did not. I found a workbook at Barnes and Noble. They had books for every grade, *What a First Grader Needs to Know*, which included all the subjects. I bought one of those each year, and two times a week, Gilfredo would do a couple pages of each subject. He continued to love art and jiujitsu classes. I would offer him other activity options, and he seemed to say yes to everything and really stuck with each one. He added T-ball, which turned into baseball. He took hip-hop dancing and did performances. He can dance! He took piano and guitar lessons. He took acting classes and did a year of Cub Scouts. The one thing we agreed on was that Cub Scouts was not so great. We could feel the small-minded thinking that ran the group (besides one couple who did offer some amazing experiences!). We never found a homeschool group we could connect with. It was not too common where I lived. He found a great group of kids to run with in the neighborhood. They were a little older, but my son loved hanging with them. Gilfredo was very friendly too. He could go to any park or be anywhere and make a friend.

I always let him know he had options, including going to regular school. One day in the beginning of his third-grade year, he told me he wanted to check out regular school. I was shocked and unprepared. I had never looked into the schools. Since the school year had already started, we only had one choice for public school, or it had to be private. I called the private school down the street and asked if he could shadow for the day. They said yes, and we set a time. I called the public school, and they never got back to me. I dropped him off the next morning at the private school. I thought for sure he would hate staying for a full day. I picked him up at the end of the day, and he came bouncing out, all happy. *He loved it!* I was in shock but put on the happy face. We got home, and I ran into the bathroom and cried. I could not believe he wanted to go. I still feel a bit ill when I watch kids go to school, and now I would be watching my son go.

I called the private school and told them that he wanted to attend, but I mentioned that he was not vaccinated. They said they would get back to me. In the meantime, I followed up with the public school. The principal told me that we could come in together to visit. Gilfredo was happy with that option too. He already knew kids in the public school from the neighborhood. The private school got back to me and told me he could not attend without vaccinations because their insurance provider would not allow it. I was shocked. I thought private school would let you have choices since you were paying tuition. The public school ended up being super helpful. They told me to go to a medical care facility for his physical, then sign a waiver taking responsibility for him not having vaccines. I thought, *Here we go into the sheep world.* I hate going into medical places.

When we got to the medical facility, the nurse had us sign forms and go into the examination room. Gilfredo was in awe. At eight years old, he had never seen a place like this. *Thank God.* He looked at me crazily when the nurse began to run tests on him, especially the eye exam, but he followed her instructions. *Welcome to another reality, son.* Everything seemed easy until the physician's assistant came in to finish up. He asked who our regular pediatrician was. I told him we did not have one. He flipped out and told me that is not how things were done around there. I told him it is in my world! He took the school papers, whited out the marks the nurse had made, and handed them back to me. He said he would not sign off on the papers. I could have choked the idiot, but I remained calm, and we left.

We went straight to the school and told them what happened. The secretary told me to go to a different medical facility that she recommended. We went to that location as I braced myself for more of the same treatment. I was pleasantly surprised. The nurse took us in the exam room and told me that if she knew what she knew about vaccinations, after all her years in practice as a nurse, she would not have vaccinated her children. She also told me that her sister homeschooled her children and they were always more advanced. She praised me for sticking to my principles. We went back to the school with the papers and went to see the school nurse. She reviewed his paperwork and said, "So, he's not vaccinated? I bet he has never been sick; I see the correlation as a nurse." I said, "No, he is rarely sick." I was so glad to find people in the mainstream world who were waking up.

I discovered the books on law of attraction by Abraham Hicks while I was pregnant. I had figured out a great deal about what was described in those books about healing on my own. It was the first time I had someone else state exactly what I was experiencing as a chiropractor and in my own healing journey. I knew there was no disease except the fact that we believed in it. Healing myself and then learning about the medical paradigm disproved all its credibility to me. Learning and experiencing the chiropractic world led me to healing and a different realm of vibration. I knew our thoughts created what happened with our bodies. We are only energy. I do not care what label the medics slap on the symptoms. I know once people lose their fear of the label, or find happiness and purpose in their life, they can heal. Not only did these books say that, but they spread that concept to every area in our lives. I knew these books came into my life at the same time as my son for a reason. They explain when you feel good and think happy thoughts, you line up with whatever you need in life. I watched this play out with my son all the time.

Now it was happening for him with school, a topic I have a lot of resistance to. My son had a magical third-grade year. He had a young man as a teacher whom he absolutely adored. He had a reading teacher whom he loved. He had friends right away, and he loved his school routine. I went to the first teacher conference, and they asked me what I had been doing with Gilfredo. They said he had such a passion to learn and was such a big thinker. They wished they could get all their students to be like that. I explained how I just let him be who he was, and I got out of the way. We would all be this brilliant if we were left to follow our own guidance. I was concerned that I was going to get scolded for him not being able to read yet. I never pushed him because I wanted him to like it. He had decided to go to school before I got him up to speed. His teachers told me not to worry, that was the easy part for them. The foundation I gave him, they could not have given. They were so inspired, and it was such a great meeting. My son was amazing everyone. I was hugely impressed by the entire faculty that ran the school. These people really cared about their students.

Within a week of my son attending school, I received a call from the vice principal. He told me someone bullied my son. I was not concerned; I knew that was part of the school environment and he would have to learn to handle himself. My mouth dropped open when the vice principal told me they already talked to my son and the bully and handled it. *Wow, that was quick and impressive.* When I saw Gilfredo after school, he was not even phased about the kid who had bullied him. He said the kid was an idiot and he was fine. He continued to thrive all year. Near the end of the school year, he began to look a bit tired from the schedule. He mentioned maybe he should go back to homeschooling after third grade. I actually encouraged him to stay because I thought he enjoyed too many things about it. He went back for fourth grade, but it was not the same. The class size grew from eighteen kids in the class to twenty-seven kids, making it hard for any teacher. My son was having to deal with the chaos of that daily. Within a month of starting the new school year, he said he was ready to leave. I told him to know for sure because he should not just keep going in and out of school. I suggested to give it until winter break and then decide. He agreed. He excelled for those few months and got all As, and when winter break came around, he was ready to leave. We went back to homeschool.

·☙·

CHAPTER 7

TAKING A NEW DIRECTION

I t was a two-year process after my son was born, that I fell out of my grace state and then got back into it, but it was remembering that space that allowed me to make it through those couple years. I was in survival mode after I had my son. I felt out of myself, my relationship was falling apart, and I was just trying to put one foot in front of the other. At the same time, the entire economy began to fall. I always find this so symbolic. My inner world was crashing just like the outer markets. The years of feeling like I never had enough all came to a head when I actually did not have enough to pay my bills. I could barely keep my head above water. It was such an awakening time. After a year of survival mode, I found the Sedona method. It was a course on releasing I could take at home with CDs, a workbook, and book. It helped release negative emotions, and boy did I have a lot. I did the lessons for six months, and it brought me to a level of peace. Not quite the grace state, but peace was good. It was interesting when my partner asked me if I was cheating on him during that time. I realized he knew something had changed because I was not fighting him anymore. Once I found my peace, I was truly unattached to any drama. I could breathe again within, only to find myself stuck with a bunch of real estate properties that I desperately needed to rebalance and had never gotten the chance to. I was spinning my wheels for a few years, trying to figure out what to do in an economic market that was not in my favor.

In the meantime, my good friend and fellow chiropractor asked me to take a look at a business opportunity with a network marketing company. She said it was the Rich Dad asset we were looking for and it embraced our holistic philosophy. I really could not handle one more thing in my life, but once I saw the opportunity, I knew I could not refuse. I jumped in, and what I discovered was all the training and mentoring I had been looking for to create financial freedom. I even found the help I needed to untangle myself from all the properties. My upline in the company was the one who gave me the direction I required to sell the properties that were financially and emotionally draining me. She had built a successful organization, had rental properties with her husband, and had the financial wisdom to guide me toward my next steps. I will never forget that. I was so impressed with her knowledge. I had no one in my life who knew what to do. I remember another family in my neighborhood told me they wanted to move. However, they decided to wait until the market came back to sell the house they lived in because they did not want to wreck their credit. I was amazed at the lack of vision they had. It was such a middle-class working mind-set without any financial wisdom at all. Most of the people around me where just like this. I wanted more for myself and my son.

I had a lot of factors coming together in my mind. My son had family from his dad's side in Miami, so we visited there a few times. I had visited prior to that with my girlfriends for vacation, and I always loved it. I originally found Miami Beach on a layover from one of my Brazil trips. We landed at 6:00 a.m. from Sao Paolo and took a taxi to spend the day on the beach before getting our connector flight to Philadelphia at 8:00 p.m. that night. I remember getting in the ocean first thing in the morning. The ocean was crystal clear, and the weather was perfect. No one was around, and it was magic swimming in the ocean. Then I ate the best breakfast at News Café and spent the entire day relaxing on the beach. Now, years later, I kept feeling a pull to move there. I wanted to close my chiropractic practice, and I felt guilty. I also realized how much I was in Delaware for the wrong reasons. I thought I had to be where my family was, but now my vision was expanding. I felt stuck in my life, with the properties and my relationships. I knew it was a symptom of an underlying pattern within myself that was related to codependency, lack, unworthiness, suffering, and struggle. I could see how those were where my normal vibrations resided, and I was not going to settle for that. Again, it is not always clear to find the invisible web that binds you, but once you do, it is so empowering. I was not quite sure how to change it, but awareness was the first step. I wanted to get rid of everything I owned in Delaware, move to Miami, and only take my son and my network marketing business with me.

I had expanded so much. I knew I could help more people with my network marketing business than through chiropractic. If you really want to evolve as a person, you need to do the work to change your vibration. I knew my network marketing company was an arena that anyone could jump into and do that work. It was like one day a lightning bolt struck me, and I knew exactly what I now wanted, and it took my breath away. *How am I ever going to do that?* I had changed and evolved as a person, but I had built my life in a way that was no longer serving me. I tried to process this inner revelation for a year and make my Delaware life work, including my practice, my properties, and my network marketing business. I am always amazed when people hit an inner blocker and give up on their dreams. I had so many different inner blockers hit me all at once. The transformation happens walking through each one. I see people give up way too often, building their own business, on their healing journey, or in making any life changes. How can you give up and act like it never happened? They are missing out.

After a year of processing my call to Miami, I began taking steps toward it. I put the properties for sale one at a time. Some had to be sold through a short sale because the value of the property was less than what I owed the mortgage company. There is a time and place for rental properties. If you have a boatload of cash and need a tax shelter with cash flow, rental properties are great. It is important to get in at the right timing of the wealth cycle. I never figured that out until the market crashed and I realized I bought in high tide. It was three years after the crash, and I did not even understand how badly it had crashed until I had the Realtor's appraisal. I was afraid of trying to sell those properties, upsetting my tenants, and losing their rental payments before they sold. It was all so complicated.

I started with the property in New Jersey. The tenants who lived there were sloppy, which did not help showing the property. It was on the market for a year when Hurricane Sandy hit. It wiped out the basement, including the heater and hot water tank. I had just put in a new hot water tank that year. I was so tired and emotionally drained, and now I had to figure this out. I heard the government was going to help, and I could apply for their relief funds. I called my insurance. Even my mortgage company sent a letter that they would work with me with payments. My cash flow was so tight, and now I could not collect rent because the building was uninhabitable without heat or hot water. I called the mortgage company, and they said I could have a grace period of maybe ninety days to delay payments. I did not pay that month as I figured out my next steps. In the meantime, the collections department from the same mortgage company started calling me about a delinquent payment. *What the hell.*

Now the insurance company was another joke. The hurricane happened the last week in October just as the weather was turning into winter. The insurance company told me that I had to have someone living in the building or it would not be covered. *Okay, now I am between a rock and a hard place.* I was learning to play their evil game. I told them someone was living there. They proceeded to go through all their nonsense red tape procedures and never paid for the heater or hot water tank replacement until the last week in January. Guess what? By the third week in January, the pipes froze. The flood insurance company told me I had to file a claim with the regular insurance for that to be covered. What the freak kind of system do we live in? I swear people are robots going around doing what they are told. Are you alive at all? Do you see what you do for a living? This is what I call ultimate sheep mode. Six thousand dollars later of regular insurance payouts, and the pipes were fixed. Then the heater and hot water tank got replaced along with everything that was water damaged in the basement after they let it sit there for more than three months. It took another year to finally sell the property for less than what I bought it for ten years earlier.

The property in Florida that I bought with two partners through the real estate investing courses went belly-up. I had to help keep paying for the construction of that property for months while the market crashed. I proceeded to go through negotiations for a short sale. I lost money and got a ding in my perfect credit. Through a Realtor, I found a buyer who made an offer on the property at the current value of the market, and we submitted it to the bank. It took about six months for the bank to approve it. Why does it take six months? *Sheep mode systems.* In the meantime, you as the owner must stop payments on your mortgage; otherwise the bank will not negotiate a short sale. Their collections department proceeds to call and harass you about why you are not making your mortgage payment during the six months that they take to sign off on your sale. Your credit goes to hell during that time until it is marked settled. My credit card companies proceeded to cut my lines of credit because of the payment delinquency to the mortgage company even though I made regular, on-time payments to them. Remember, as we the little people went through this nightmare, the government bailed out trillions of dollars to the banks that in turn becomes a hidden tax (inflation) for us. Funny how people want the government to help. *Wake up.*

The small townhouse I bought had its own drama. During the same hurricane, the storm water surge created another dynamic. The sewer backed up into the basement of that property, and I was told the city was responsible for stopping it. I kept calling, without being able to reach anyone for a long time. When I finally did, they told me they could not do anything. I decided to call the fire department. They came and called the city; the city finally listened and took care of the problem. The city was one of the worst to deal with. This was not my first rodeo with them. They were always in ignorance mode. The sewer incident happened on Wednesday afternoon, October 31st, I was trying to enjoy mall day with my son when I got that call from my tenant. I was calling the city and the fire department from the mall. We got ourselves into the car, and I brought Gilfredo to his dad. I raced off to the property, which took until almost 8:00 p.m. to get under control, as I was missing Halloween with my son. Missing Halloween with my son killed me the most. I never miss anything with him. His dad took him through the neighborhood, but when I got back, I made him go for round two with me. He was tired, but we had fun.

In the meantime, my office building was giving me more problems. I had a new tenant who wanted to open a business in my building. She went to get the permits from the town, and it opened up Pandora's box. The town decided I did not have enough parking, but I could be grandfathered in because of the age of the building. However, that would take a few months to go through, which would delay my tenant's opening. The town also decided that my building was not being taxed enough because it was four units versus three. I never built out or changed the square footage of the building. They could take three months to hold up my tenant's business but could just double my property taxes immediately. *Unbelievable.* I hope people think about this: our taxes are paying for all these government positions, and many could be done away with. We are paying them to enslave us. There is so much wasted time and so many senseless jobs choking up the system. Also, do you remember I bought my own house in May 2006 from Countrywide, fully financed? Well, I finally sold it as a short sale in January 2014 for $60,000 less than what I paid for it. Seven years of payments and repairs, all for nothing. Still think it is an investment to own a house? Even if I had put the 20 percent down, it would have evaporated into thin air unless I did not sell it for many more years. How many years more would it have taken to just get to the amount I paid for it?

CHAPTER 8

MADE IT TO MIAMI!

I searched out apartments on different trips to Miami, and then I continued that search online. On one trip back home from Miami, my son and I were waiting to board our flight to Philadelphia. I noticed this wild-looking woman, eccentrically dressed, talking loudly on her phone. When we boarded the plane, I was sitting in my seat, and I saw her walking down the aisle. I was thinking to myself, *Oh please do not let her sit next me,* as she sat down next to me. She ended up entertaining Gilfredo and me with her stories of her move to Miami from Philadelphia. She was going back to visit family. She loved Miami, and she recommended an apartment complex in South Beach. As she said it, I got tingles all over my body that this was the place I was supposed to live. I went home and searched it online. Then I saw it in person, on one more Miami trip, before we finally moved. I did not understand Miami from Miami Beach or any other section in South Florida before I moved.

Once I arrived and got settled in, I felt like I had come

home. It was so easy for me to adjust to life in Miami Beach. I loved the people, the diversity, the cultures, the vibe, and the events, and I knew I was in my exact place. My apartment, my view, and my location were perfect. Everything felt like divine order. I was still struggling to figure out what having a life looked like, and now I was beginning to understand. My soul came vibrantly alive in this city. I did not know I had so many interests and that I liked going to so many networking events and meeting so many open-minded people. My inner guidance had been guiding me all along the way. What if I had not listened? It took a leap of faith to move here, and it became so much more than I could have ever imagined.

Building my network marketing business has been so much more to me than I ever dreamed too. It has been so much about personal development and becoming who you personally need to be in order to receive the money, the promotion, or the team. Anyone can do this business, but we are all unique individuals with different strengths, weaknesses, talents, and backgrounds. Therefore, everyone's journey to build this business will look different even if we follow the same success plan. I will say that I had to revamp my entire being to get what I dreamed of with my business, and I still have so much further to go. I carried so much poverty consciousness and struggle that I had to learn to go out, enjoy life, and meet people. This has been a complete rewiring in my brain that was extremely uncomfortable in the beginning.

I needed a reason to socialize. It is great to make friends, but my conversations become extremely limited with people. My son once reminded me that I am not normal as he listed all the things I do not believe in: disease, religion, marriage, school, and government. So many of these institutions have disempowered us as individuals. I think everyone has a right to live the way they choose, but I will not sit around complaining about problems when I have found so many solutions. I want to be around people who are ready to change their lives or are actively doing it. Sadly, it is an exceedingly small percent that actually want to change their lives. I do not understand this. You can be, do, or have anything you want! Why would you settle for less? Why would you fight for your limitations? Trust me when I tell you that having the courage to walk through the fears that bind you is the most rewarding part of the journey. It makes you stronger, wiser, more peaceful, and more blissful.

By the time my son was in sixth grade, I began to unschool. When I had to relearn what that grade was teaching, I knew he did not need it, so we began developing our own path even more. It is criminal that none of us get financial education in school. I believe there is a reason for this. It keeps people enslaved to the system. There is no reason why all of us cannot be financially free, peaceful, healthy, abundant, and independent. I honestly believe it is our birthright. My plan all along was for my son to be financially independent, so that he has choices in life and the freedom to live by his own design.

This pushed me to begin investigating how to invest a bit deeper because now my son was at an age that I could teach him. I was still confused myself. I did not like saving part of my money and giving it to some broker to diversify for the long term. I needed to know more. I began reading about Warren Buffet. I read Benjamin Graham. I studied the Buffettology books that describe how to value invest like Buffett. I knew they never fixed a very messed-up system from when the economy crashed in 2008. In my gut, I felt something was wrong. A few things emerged into my life simultaneously. What is the saying? When the student is ready, the teacher appears? At three different networking events, I was led to my next steps. One recommendation was the book *Dark Money* by Jane Mayer, about how the very wealthy form groups that influence the way the laws are passed, not for the good of the people but for their own personal and financial controls. Next, I kept hearing the term *Bitcoin*, so I found a book to learn more. Finally, someone recommended to me the *Hidden Secrets of Money* YouTube series by Mike Maloney. He was a Rich Dad advisor, so I paid even more attention. All these things began connecting dots that led me to further information, molding my understanding of our economic system and how to invest.

Dark Money discussed how billionaires are influencing the system to gain personal power and control. That was not hard for me to believe because I always knew on some level that to see the underlying vision on anything, you have to follow the money trail. This just proved it. I read *How Money Got Free* by Brian Patrick Eha about Bitcoin. It made total sense. I remember how the internet came in and changed the way we got information and how we communicated. I could correlate how Bitcoin, other cryptocurrencies, and the blockchain technology could revamp how we exchange currencies. I had read *The Creature from Jekyll Island* by G. Edward Griffin about how the Federal Reserve was formed by a private banking cartel who corrupted our banking systems here in the US. I didn't know what to do with that information when I read it years prior, but as I learned about cryptocurrencies, I remembered that book and how this new technology could free us from the chains of slavery we are under. The *Hidden Secrets of Money* YouTube series explain the wealth cycles of money and the rise and fall of different empires. I could see that the US was on the brink of collapse. This connected so many dots about what I had experienced, especially since 2008. These are the things I began sharing with my son.

I remember talking with a teacher I met at a networking event about what a shame it is that we do not get financial skills in school. She said, "Yes, I agree with you. Students should learn about balancing their checkbook." *What?* I was horrified she said that to me. This was her idea of financial education. Sadly, I am finding this is the average person's idea of financial education. I am referring to building wealth with assets and residual income. We should be learning Austrian economics, free markets, and capitalist economy. We ought to understand how the Federal Reserve banking system is printing money whenever it wants, causing a silent tax called inflation. That keeps the cost of living rising to the point that people cannot afford to support themselves by working. Then, enforce an income tax to pay for the Fed's criminal activity. It deeply bothers me that so many children go unfed unless they are in school. Why are there this many families living in poverty? Why is this happening in our country? They are destroying our economy and brainwashing us into believing they do it for the people. Did you know there are many now speaking up about how income tax is not in the Constitution? The Federal Reserve system is based on Keynesian economics, which was based on Marxism and Communism. No wonder they propagate how criminal capitalism is without government intervention. Austrian economics is based on a free economy where supply and demand naturally regulate themselves without the big booms and busts that government intervention brings. This led me to read *Economics in One Lesson* by Henry Hazlitt. It explained so much.

It reminded me of chiropractic school when I learned how medical intervention interferes with the body's own ability to heal itself, yet they have propagated the masses to believe they have to go to the doctor to be well. People will argue that they need the medicine. Well, the third leading cause of death is from medical intervention. You decide. I see how the government's regulations continue to cause so much harm to our economy, just like the medical profession does. Lightbulbs lit up all over my brain. We have been programmed for enslavement in so many ways to the point that people beg for their own enslavement.

I found Jeff Berwick and The Dollar Vigilante on YouTube. The first video I saw was Berwick speaking about being against vaccines, circumcision, and schools. He was speaking my language, so I had to continue listening. He spoke of how governments are criminal systems to control the people; he was an anarchist. There is a misunderstanding of what anarchy is. It is not being a violent person causing harm to other people and property, as what happens in riots. An anarchist believes in the right to live his or her own life without government intervention. The belief is that natural order and peace would follow in society, just as the symptoms of an unjust society come from too much government. He also spoke about how the Fed's continuous printing of money is devaluing the dollar; hence he formed The Dollar Vigilante to help people rise and prosper during its collapse. He spoke of how free markets prosper and calls himself an anarcho-capitalist. This made sense to me. I listened to his videos for about six months before I became a subscriber so I could really learn how to invest in today's world, and it has been amazing. My son does it with me. I wish I could have learned this when I was his age. Listening to Jeff Berwick led me to Dr. Ron Paul, Doug Casey, and David Icke. I read all their newsletters and books and watch their videos. What an education. I am beyond ecstatic that I found this for myself but especially for my son. It is all exactly what I had been looking for. Empowerment!

This feeling of empowerment reminds me of what I experienced healing myself, practicing as a chiropractor, and finding my grace state. Abraham Hicks says do what makes you happy. When you condition yourself to follow your bliss, it leads you to your greatest good. This sounds so simple, but look how we have been programmed all our lives, not to listen to ourselves. It is super important to begin to train yourself to be happy. The life force that runs your body flows optimally when you are happy—and not just superficially happy where you keep yourself busy with travel, shopping, going out all the time, and drinking. I did that too. There is nothing wrong with those things, but that is not the happiness I am talking about. It is about finding peace within yourself that you can just be. It is about finding a purpose in your life that you contribute to others. It is about appreciating the small moments in your day.

Appreciation is a great place to start. I began a gratitude journal when I first opened my practice. I would write down at least five things I was grateful for every day. Those five things turned into twenty things. I have been journaling since I was eleven years old. I had my gratitude journal separate. I noticed in my regular journal I would complain. As my vibration began to rise and my focus turned to things to be grateful for, I decided to journal all the great things that happened during my day, combining my gratitude journal with my regular journal. My days kept getting better and better. As I moved through different experiences in my life, if the darkness showed up, the releasing techniques really worked. I recommend the Sedona method. If you can learn to honor where you are within every moment of your day, you can find the guidance on what you need to do next.

Abraham Hicks always says to find relief. If something has you upset or stuck, take a walk, take a nap, read a good book, or take a breather. Once you allow yourself that break, you will receive inspiration for your next steps. It really is that simple. The hard part is untangling all the scenarios in your life that you created from societal programming and not from the place of true alignment with yourself. The more people there are following their bliss, following their inner guidance, and creating their lives from happiness and empowerment, the more we will radically change the world. I read *Power vs Force* by David Hawkins. Hawkins talks about the hundredth monkey syndrome. The study was done observing monkeys. The concept is when one person deviates from the mainstream mind-set, it looks weird. It becomes accepted as normal once the hundredth person begins to accept this new mind-set. Also, Hawkins says that one person in their alignment can counteract millions who are not. The time is now!

I fell in love with my network marketing business because I found it to be a simple vehicle that anyone can incorporate into their busy life where they can work on their health, their wealth, and their mind-set. As a chiropractor, I could adjust you all day long, but if your lifestyle is in the rat race, you will never have true well-being. You must learn to align yourself to your inner guidance. You must get in tune with yourself and become the owner of your life. This would align to the anarchist perspective. The journey to getting in tune with yourself is the transformative process. I love Jim Rohn's quote, "Everyone should become a millionaire, not for the money, but for who they become in the process." I could not agree more. You have to do the work to heal yourself and build your empire and own your mind-set because it is in doing the work that you discover your power.

CHAPTER 9

RECOMMENDATIONS FOR CREATING YOUR DESIRED LIFE — PULLING IT ALL TOGETHER

E veryone is in a different place in their life and experiencing different things. I do believe we are all the same in needing health, financial peace, mental peace, happy relationships, and joy. My brain thinks differently from the mainstream, so this is how I navigate my life and advice I would give to a friend. The best place to start is to honor where you are. Next is to learn to practice getting in tune with your intuition. That is your inner wisdom, and once you get used to following it, it is magic. I would get a blank notebook and start writing out how you want your life to be. Ask yourself, where will I be in five years if I keep doing what I am doing in every area of my life? If you do not have a clear vision yet, that is okay. Start by making lists of all the things you appreciate in your life. Make lists of all the things that make you happy or inspire you. Make these lists a daily habit. It begins to program your mind to notice all these positive aspects. The more you notice them, the more you attract these things into your life.

The life force that is flowing in you is Source energy or God energy or whatever you prefer to call it. The universal intelligence that runs the world (makes the sun come up every day) is the same power that runs your body. Think about how powerful that is! Your heart beats and your lungs breathe without you having to do it, along with so many millions of other functions. That life force is at its optimum flow when you are happy and expanded as a person. When you are in fear or in stress, you contract and slow your flow a bit. Ever notice that? That is a huge awareness once you start to connect those dots. Think about how many things affect your stress or happiness level on a daily basis. The process is to start making your happiness bigger than your stress. It is not to say that you will not have things that will stress you out. Stress is a part of life, and it is what helps us evolve. The problem is that most of us have been trained to live in a constant stressed state, ignore our happiness, and accept certain norms as the way life has to be. I hope this process makes you dig deep and think outside the box to find your own normal. We are energetic beings, and once you learn to adjust your frequency, you can become the magnetic creator you were meant to be!

The key to health is to become in tune with your own energetic frequency. Things that drain you in life will literally drain your energy and cause you to enter a dis-eased state. The mainstream has all kinds of names for this dis-eased state. We have become trained to believe in those disease labels and give over our power to them. We lose focus on the power that runs the body, and we begin focusing on the disease. The fear of the disease drains your energy, weakens your immune system, and actually creates more of the diseased tissue even if the diagnosis were a moment in time, and maybe would have cleared itself without the diagnosis.

Another example is if you are going to a job that you hate every day, you are draining your energy. If you do not figure out a plan B, you may very well get a diagnosis that will wake you up. Not only are you draining your energy chronically, but the diagnosis gives you a reason to not deal with your job issue. Now you are forced to make a change in your life, but it may not be what you would choose if you were fully conscious of the decision. See the connection? Once you start to connect the dots in your life as a whole, you will no longer be able to compartmentalize your life. It is a whole, and it works together.

You have to start where you are and with where your beliefs lie. If you feel secure going to a medical doctor, then you should go. But know that they are only trained in giving drugs or performing surgery. The medical paradigm has been run by the pharmaceutical industry for years now. Gone is the small-town doctor who makes house visits and knows you and your lifestyle as a whole person. The more specialized the doctor, the further away they get from viewing the person as a whole. I feel that you open Pandora's box by going to the medical doctor. If they label you with a disease, that is a huge auto-suggestion that they implant in your mind. I believe the one main blocker that does not allow people to heal is their fear of the disease. If you were labeled with a disease, bless it. Anything can heal!

Use this disease as a gift to get in tune with your body, your mind, and your life. It can be the most empowering thing that can happen to you. I am amazed that people get a diagnosis, then think it's normal to take a drug and fill their body with chemical poisons, without ever making any changes to their everyday life, such as cleaning out toxins in their diet, products, and mind. Then they pray and hope the doctor gives them a clean bill of health on their next visit. Get all the information you can from the medical doctor, but take it as an opinion and then go on a mission to find out all other kinds of information. Start listening to what your gut guides you to do. Small, baby steps, day by day. You do not have to figure it all out right away. Embrace the journey.

The medical world screwed up my spine and left me sick, and then for five years they had no idea how to help me get better. I am thankful for this because I figured out how to heal myself and lost all fear of disease. I wish for everyone to see health the way I see it. Everyone would be so empowered, and we would have an extremely healthy world. It is important to read things and watch videos to learn about how your body heals. I love Louise Hay, Dr. Joe Dispenza, Dr. Bruce Lipton, and Anita Moorjani. I will put all this information in the suggested reading at the end of the book.

Going through my dad's death as a young girl was also a huge blessing. I feel my dad's spiritual guidance all the time. I know I grew more as a person from my dad through his death than if he were to have raised me here on the physical plain. His death released me from any fear about dying. He blessed me with looking for a reason to live. That perspective has guided me to an amazing life. Choose how you view what happens to you in your life. Look for the gift in every scenario. You can either play victim to your life circumstances or use it to propel you into your greatness.

I believe it is important to get rid of the toxins you have been ingesting and putting on your body. Our food had been so processed and chemicalized that it has become more toxic than nutritious. It is important to buy organic and natural products as much as you can. Imagine how hard your body has to work to unload all those harmful toxins if it is coming in contact with them all day every day. That is another reason the body breaks down; it is not natural for it to come into contact with that many harmful chemicals on a daily basis—not only with the foods we ingest but with the products we put on our skin. The US only bans eleven harmful chemicals from our products. Europe bans fourteen hundred harmful chemicals. Those chemicals in our soaps, cleansers, makeup, and lotions go directly into our bloodstream through the skin, which is our largest organ.

One of the many reasons I chose to build a business with my network marketing company is because the products are plant based and free of harmful toxins. With this company, I can share a synergistic and holistic approach to healthy living inside and out, including an amazing 30 Days to Healthy Living program that educates people to live a clean lifestyle. It makes it so simple. I am proud this company puts the well-being of people and the planet as their top priority. It is important that we invest in companies like this for a sustainable and thriving future. We vote every time we make a purchase; make sure it is a company that you believe in. Even your household cleaners and laundry detergents need to be nontoxic. Once you clear the majority of chemicals from your daily life, you will begin to be in tune with your body even more. Symptoms and unnatural cravings will subside. You will learn how certain foods affect you. You will feel your natural cravings so your body can guide you in every meal, telling you what it needs in each moment. Finding this freedom and rhythm with eating is so empowering.

It is really important to be mindful throughout your day. The thoughts you think are creating your reality. Become aware of how you are feeling each moment. Question things. Why are you eating: stress or hunger? Are you fulfilled in your life? Are you at a job that makes you feel purpose? If not, it is critical that you make a new plan. Are your relationships authentic? Can you be your true self with the people around you, including family? Just because they are family does not mean you have to subject yourself to a toxic environment. Set a new standard. You set the boundary for how people treat you. This is by no means an easy thing to do. Small steps.

Journal how you envision your life, including the people. Sometimes it has to be an internal vision written only on paper before you begin to act on these things. I do believe that once you get clear on what you want, you will be guided to your next step. It is amazing how many toxic relationships we engage in because we think it is normal. Once you shift that and create a new normal with positive relationships, you will wonder how you ever settled for less. You have to be okay by yourself. You can jump from one partner to the next to not be alone. However, this can be a bad habit. If you do not have a good relationship with yourself, you will never have a good relationship with someone else. That high that you feel from falling in love is the high that you can feel in your normal daily life by yourself. Your life can feel like bliss every day. Even when things bother you, they quickly resolve themselves into something better when you live in a raised frequency. Disease and accidents are a low-vibrational frequency. Practice raising your vibrational frequency and watch how magical your life can be.

Let us talk money! Having a job can be a great place to start, especially if you love what you do, but a job can keep you just over broke. Having a financial plan is different from having a job. You need to create a plan where you put your money into assets that create residual income. This takes figuring out on your own because none of this is taught in school. Even economics taught at universities are based on Keynesian economics, which is based on Marxism, socialism, fascism, and Communism. It is what the Federal Reserve bank that runs our US government is based on. We do not have a free capitalist market like they say, where they choose to blame all the problems. The problems are coming from too many corrupt people in power and too much out-of-control government. Austrian economics are based on a totally free market of supply and demand. Dr. Ron Paul's books and the Mises Institute are excellent resources on this.

Rich Dad Poor Dad is a must read to understand creating financial freedom and asset income. The *Hidden Secrets of Money* series is important to understand the wealth cycles of the economy in order to know how, when, and where to invest. This is what I was clueless about when I purchased all my real estate at the top of a government-created bubble, and when it all came crashing down. Some asset incomes are rental real estate, value stocks, building a business you can take to the stock market, and network marketing. Important insurances against the value of the dollar are precious metals such as gold and silver, and cryptocurrencies such as Bitcoin and Monero. I highly recommend The Dollar Vigilante on these topics. Start learning about all these different avenues. Find out where the economic wealth cycle is when you start and then plan on how you want to begin, until you build yourself multiple streams of income. Financial freedom is when you have enough asset income coming in every month to pay your bills and your preferred lifestyle, and you have the time freedom to choose how you spend your day. This takes time to learn, along with different skills and a new mind-set. Again, ask yourself where you will be in five years if you keep doing what you are doing.

I have spent my adult life trying to wake people up. As a chiropractor, I have seen people continually make decisions that really are not about long-term health but more of a quick fix. As a network marketer, I see people ignore me or tell me they are too busy to learn to create residual income even when they have no plan for building wealth. I have been angry most of my young life, knowing that what we consider normal life is not working. I had to retrain myself to own my health, to own my wealth, to own my mind-set, and to own my happiness. I hate seeing people play victims in their lives. It was not until the most recent crisis that I could really see how we have been under a hypnotism to be dependent on our school, medical, and government systems. None of these systems empower us. They enslave our minds to be victims in our lives, waiting for someone to tell us what to do. I hope more people wake up to the negative programming they have had and take back their power. We are love—and not a small, conditional love but a big, powerful, unconditional love! We have everything we need to be, do, or have whatever we want in life. We must raise ourselves up from the programming and start thinking outside of the box. We have to learn to raise our vibrations to become the magnificent creators we were born to be!

Recommended Books, Videos, and other Sources

You Can Heal Your Body by Louise Hay
You Can Heal Your Life by Louise Hay
Dying to Be Me by Anita Moorjani
You Are the Placebo by Dr. Joe Dispenza (Any of his books, videos, or seminars)
Ask and It Is Given by Abraham Hicks (Any of their books, videos, or seminars)
Seth Speaks by Jane Roberts
The Power of the Imagination by Neville Goddard
The Complete Works by Florence Scovel Shinn
Autobiography of a Yogi by Paramahansa Yogananda
The Gift, Poems by Hafiz, Translations by Daniel Ladinsky
The Essential Rumi, Translations by Coleman Barks with John Moyne
The Sedona Method by Hale Dwoskin
Codependent No More by Melody Beattie
Take Off Your Glasses and See by Dr. Jacob Liberman, D.O., Ph.D.

Monumental Myths of the Modern Medical Mafia by Ty
    Bollinger,
    @thetruthaboutvaccinesttav,
    @thetruthaboutcancerttac
Dr. Sherri Tenpenny: Vaxxter.com, @drtenpenny
ChildrensHealthDefense.org by Robert F. Kennedy, Jr.,
    @childrenshealthdefense
National Vaccine Information Center: nvic.org
    @vaccinefreedom
Dr. Rashid A. Buttar (YouTube)
Bruce H. Lipton, Ph.D. (YouTube)
Kelly Brogan, MD @kellybroganmd
Power vs. Force by David Hawkins
Rich Dad Poor Dad by Robert Kiyosaki
The Business of the 21st Century by Robert Kiyosaki
The Four Year Career by Richard Bliss Brooke
Mach 2 with you Hair on Fire by Richard Bliss Brooke
The Snowball, Warren Buffett and the Business of Life by Alice
    Schroeder
The Intelligent Investor by Benjamin Graham
The New Buffettology by Mary Buffett and David Clark
The Creature from Jekyll Island by G. Edward Griffin
Gold & Silver by Mike Maloney
Hidden Secrets of Money (YouTube video series) by Mike
    Maloney
GoldSilver (W/Mike Maloney) (YouTube)
Right on the Money by Doug Casey
International Man newsletters by Doug Casey via email
Nomad Capitalist by Andrew Henderson
Economics in One Lesson by Henry Hazlitt
The Revolution by Dr. Ron Paul

End the Fed by Dr. Ron Paul
Ron Paul Liberty Report (YouTube)
Mises Institute: mises.org
The Dollar Vigilante by Jeff Berwick (YouTube)
Really Graceful (YouTube)
Everything You Need to Know by David Icke
The Trigger by David Icke
The Most Dangerous Superstition by Larken Rose
Dark Money by Jane Mayer
How Money Got Free by Brian Patrick Eha

9 781982 255138